General editor, Nuffield Home Economics
Marie Edwards

Editors of this book
Marie Edwards
Sandra Lowry

Authors of this book
Richard C. Brierley
Fran Challis
Sarah Codrington
Anne Constable
Marie Edwards
Elizabeth Fenwick
Ralph Hancock
Sandra Lowry
Anne Miller
Pauline Swaine
Arthur Tarrant
Peter Wood
Wilf Woodhead

Contributors to the Background reading
William Anderson
Richard C. Brierley
Krysia Brochocka
John Burton
Sarah Codrington
Bruce Cowen
Elaine Drummond
Ralph Hancock
Frank Kitson
Julia McSwiney
Katrina Miller
Colin Newton
Ian Sentance
John Stewart

Organizers, Nuffield Home Economics 1977-81
Harry Faulkner
Sharon M. Mansell

The Nuffield-Chelsea Curriculum Trust would also like to thank the following for their help:

Steven Baker
Phil Connolly
J. McSavage
Suzanna Osman Jones
Beta Schofield

British Gas
Design Council
Nucleus Housing Association
St John Ambulance
Warwickshire Trading Standards Department

Nuffield Home Economics

PEOPLE AND HOMES

Published for the Nuffield-Chelsea Curriculum Trust by Hutchinson Education

Hutchinson & Co. (Publishers) Ltd
An imprint of the Hutchinson Publishing Group
17—21 Conway Street, London W1P 6JD

Hutchinson Group (Australia) Pty Ltd
16—22 Church Street, Hawthorn, Melbourne, Victoria 3122

Hutchinson Group (NZ) Ltd
32—34 View Road, PO Box 40—086, Glenfield, Auckland 10

Hutchinson Group (SA) (Pty) Ltd
PO Box 337, Bergvlei 2012, South Africa

First published 1985

British Library Cataloguing in Publication Data
Nuffield-Chelsea Curriculum Trust
People and homes. — (Nuffield home economics).
Pupil book.
1. Home economics
I. Series
640 TX167

ISBN 0 09 152941 7

Design and art direction by Ivan Dodd

Layout by Ian Smith

Printed and bound in Great Britain by
Anchor Brendon Ltd, Tiptree, Essex.

CONTENTS

Acknowledgements

Courtesy of Abbey National: 12.18.
Barclays Bank plc: 12.6.
Barnaby's Picture Library: 14.4b, 14.5.
Bob Bray: 2.2, 2.3, 2.8, 3.2a, b, c, 3.3, 3.5, 3.7a, b, 15.22a, b. c.
Bridgeman Art Library: 10.15, 15.8.
British Gas: 8.5a, b, 8.6a, b, 8.16a, b, c.
Courtesy of Christie's: 14.4a.
Richard Davies: 6.3, 15.20.
Design Council: 15.1, 15.3a, b, 15.4, 15.5a, b, 15.6, 15.7, 15.10, 15.11, 15.12, 15.13, 15.14, 15.16, 15.18, 15.21, 15.26, 15.27.
Disabled Living Foundation: 5.5a, b.
Electricité de France: 8.2b.
Fibreglass Ltd, Insulation Division: 8.15.
Format Photographs Ltd/Maggie Murray: 2.4.
GLC Photographic Unit: 5.6a, b.
Inner London Education Authority, Learning Materials Service: 12.13a.
Frank Kitson: 6.6b, 9.16, 10.2, 10.3a, b, 10.7, 12.1, 12.17, 13.2a, b, 13.10, 13.14, 14.1, 14.2a, b, 14.10a, b, 14.11, 14.13, 15.23.
Lever Brothers Ltd: 13.8a, b, 13.12.
H. Leverton & Co. Ltd: 12.13b.
London Express News and Feature Services: 11.2b.
Manchester City Council, City Architect's Department: 15.24.
Mansell Collection: 13.9.
National Children's Home/John R. Simmons: 1.12.
R.K. Pilsbury: 7.2.
Eileen Preston: 12.13d.
Royal Society for the Prevention of Accidents: 11.4a, b, c.
Anni Silverleaf: 6.6a.
J. Smith (Southern) Ltd: 11.2a.
Thorn EMI Domestic Electrical Appliances Ltd: 13.4b.
Wilf Woodhead: 1.2, 1.3, 1.4, 1.5, 1.6, 1.7, 1.9a, b, 2.5, 2.6, 2.10, 2.11, 2.12, 3.1, 3.2d, 7.1, 7.3, 7.5b, 7.7, 7.8, 8.2a, 8.4, 8.7, 8.9, 8.10, 8.13a, b, 8.14, 9.1, 9.2, 9.3, 9.4, 9.5, 9.6, 9.7, 9.8, 9.9, 9.12, 9.13, 9.14, 10.14, 12.7, 14.6, 14.8, 14.12, 15.2, 15.25.
Zanussi Collection of Antique Household Appliances: 13.4a.

Figure 1.11 is taken from Central Statistical Service (1984) *Social trends*. Reproduced by permission of the Controller, H.M.S.O.

Illustrations by
Becky Cole, Pat McNeill,
and Taurus Graphics.
Cover illustration by
Robin Dodd.
Tables by Nina Konrad.

Introduction

What is *People and homes* about? In this book you will learn how the needs and wants of different types of people — including yourself — can be met in their homes. You will learn something about how to look after babies and young children and about people with special needs, including the elderly and the disabled.

You will think about the 'survival skills' you will need when you leave home: how to find somewhere to live, and how to organize your life successfully. In the chapter on money management you will learn how to make the best use of the resources you have and be able to pay all your bills. The chapter on choosing and buying helps you to make the choices that are right for you.

How much do you know about home maintenance? This book describes the structure of houses and the importance of energy efficiency, and introduces you to problems ranging from putting up shelves to painting the ceiling. Finally in the chapter on design you will learn more about how to create an attractive and convenient home environment for yourself.

CHAPTER 1

Making a home

1.1
WHAT IS 'HOME'?

The idea of 'home' is a very important one in our language and culture. It is not, however, a simple idea. You cannot completely define it in one short sentence. It means different things to different people. In this chapter we are going to look at some of the various meanings of the word, and what goes into making a place 'home'.

Q 1

Write your own definition of what the word 'home' means to you.
Now look up the definition of the word 'home' in at least two different sources, such as an encyclopaedia and a dictionary.

1.2
BRICKS AND MORTAR?

A good place to start is with the materials and structure of the house. When a house is first built it is not a 'home'. If you have ever been into a newly-built, unoccupied house, you will know that it doesn't feel friendly, warm, lived-in, inviting, comfortable, and dry. Quite the opposite. It feels like what it is, just a collection of materials: bricks, plaster, glass, timber, tiles, and so on, arranged in a particular way.

Of course, if you have a good imagination, you may be able to picture it in your mind as a home. How will you do this? Well, you will fill it with lots of the things that each of us think of as being associated with home: people, possessions, warmth, and

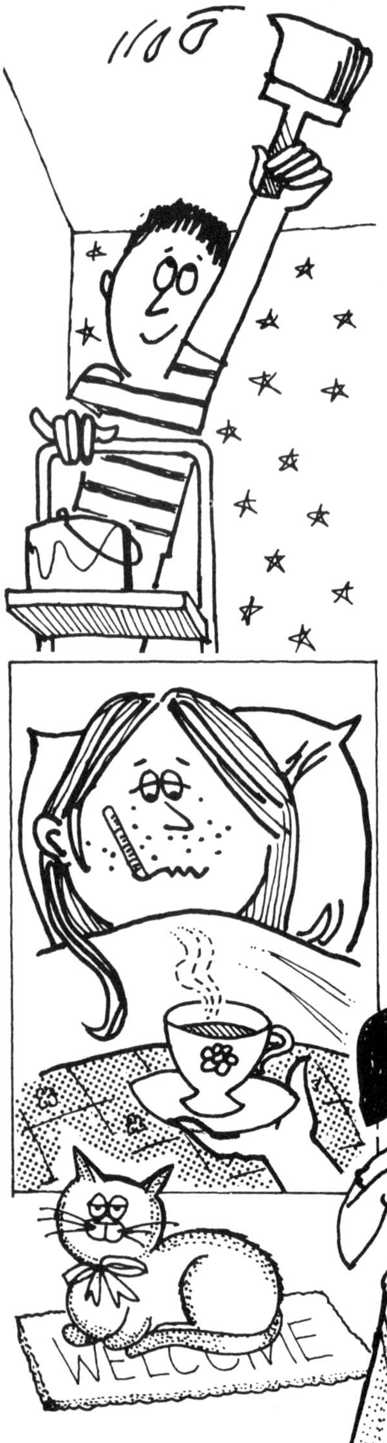

Figure 1.1

light. You will conjure up all the activities that take place in our homes, either jointly or individually. In addition to these material, physical things, perhaps you day-dream about the less substantial aspects that are implied by home: the idea of privacy, being surrounded by those you love, feeling secure and protected against the outside world, and the notion of permanence, the ability to relax without having to deal with new situations and people, the impression of familiarity, and so on.

Q 2

Discuss which are the most important things that *for you* mean that your house has become a home. Can these things be divided up into groups? Work together to classify what goes on in a home.

Before considering some of these things, let's go back for a moment to thinking about the structure of the house. Perhaps the first and most obvious consideration in how we make a home is the *design* of the house: how the materials are arranged into a particular structure of rooms, windows, stairs, and services. In a perfect world, we would all be given the opportunity to design our houses to suit our individual needs and circumstances. Of course, this hardly ever happens. Even if we did have this opportunity, the problem is that our needs and circumstances don't remain static; they change throughout our lives.

Q 3

List what you think are the major ways in which our needs and circumstances change throughout life. How do you think these changes might affect the sort of house we might need?

In practice, the physical layout of the house is almost always determined by someone else: the architect who draws the plans which the house-builder must follow. It is reasonable for us to ask how architects know what we want from our home. The answer is, of course, that architects *don't* usually know for sure. They design houses for particular 'groups' of people: the

Figure 1.2
Houseboat.

Figure 1.3
Army houses in Dorset.

elderly, first-time buyers, and so on, as well as 'family' houses. All the designs will have to provide some basic facilities which are common to people: somewhere for sleeping, eating, bathing, toilet, recreation, and storage. However, the architect cannot know in detail about the people who will live in the house, and therefore his design can only be a compromise.

Q 4
Design a bed-sit for yourself. Make sure that you have provided for all the things you listed in question 2.

When we make a house a 'home', we are doing this by imposing *our* ideas, beliefs, concerns, interests, needs, and requirements upon those which the architects must have had when they originally drew the plans. Let's now look at some of the things which make a house 'home'.

1.3
HOME IS THE PLACE WHERE I LIVE

Q 5
Look at the pictures in figures 1.2 to 1.7. What kind of people might live in each one?

Perhaps the heading for this section is the simplest description of a home. Yet the apparent simplicity covers a great variety of meanings. When we say 'the place', it suggests one single fixed permanent place. Indeed, the definitions you found in question 1 almost certainly talked of home in terms of 'a fixed residence'. However, this notion of permanence isn't necessarily part of everyone's idea of home. Many people live in temporary accommodation. We can think of families having to move around due to jobs, or perhaps families living in married quarters when the husband is a professional in the services. Students may live in halls of residence when away at college. Some people have more than one house. Some people live in caravans. For all of these people the fact that their residence is not permanent, or fixed, or single, doesn't necessarily mean that they do not think of it as home.

Figure 1.7
Flats in Casablanca.

Figure 1.4
Old people's home.

Figure 1.5
Itinerant caravan site.

Figure 1.6
College hall of residence.

Of course, 'the place' will mean different things depending upon where you are. The answer you give to the question 'where do you live?' will depend upon whether at the time you are in your own street, town, area, district, or country. The greater your distance from your actual residence the more general your answer will become. If you are abroad you may even just answer 'Britain'. There would certainly be little point in giving the house number and street name if you are thousands of miles away!

So it seems as if the idea of 'home' may not just be the particular 'fixed residence', but can become quite generalized to include even the country we live in. With this in mind we can try to identify what it is about the place where we live that makes it feel like home in this broad sense. One very important factor must of course be *familiarity*. Places feel like home when we know them well, when they don't spring surprises on us. In our home town or area we will know which way the roads go, where all the shops are, and the language or accents which the people around us speak. Just as, taking the narrower sense, in our own house we know all the rooms and what they look like, where all the light switches are, where the scissors are kept, which stair creaks, and how the people around us will behave.

Because we are so familiar with our homes we don't expect to feel ill-at-ease, cautious, unsure, or frightened in this setting. If we did, then an essential ingredient which makes us feel 'at home' would be missing.

Q 6
What is it about the area in which you live that makes it feel familiar to you? Discuss this with the others in your group and make a list of the things which each of you consider to be the most important.

Going back to our original description of a home as 'the place where I live', even the phrase 'I live' may mean lots of different things to people in different circumstances. To an elderly person who rarely goes out, life may be conducted almost entirely within the home, whereas a young person with a job and a busy social life may only use the home to sleep in and occasionally

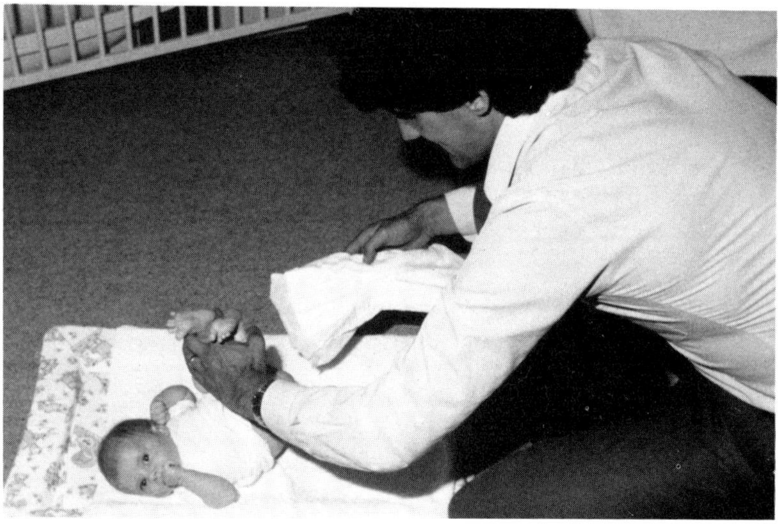

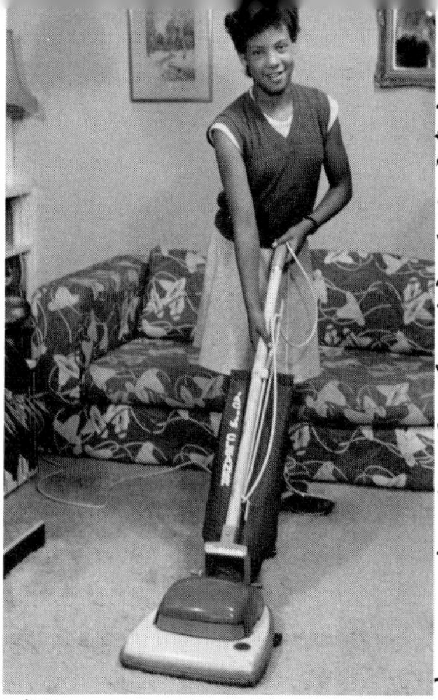

Figure 1.9

eat in. Yet both will consider that they 'live' in a particular place and call it home. For the elderly person, there is no doubt about this. For the young person, spending so few hours at home, an outside observer may not think they are really 'living' there, but merely using 'home' as a place to sleep and to keep their possessions, that is, as a base. Throughout the ages many young people must have heard the parental complaint 'you treat this place like a hotel'. What they mean is that it is not being treated like your home.

Q 7

How long does each member of your family spend at home? Take a typical weekday and estimate how many hours out of 24 each person spends within the home. Put your results in a table.

1.4
HOME IS THE PLACE WHERE I DO WHAT I WANT

Not everybody who lives at home would whole-heartedly agree with such a statement. The housewife with young children might feel that her days were spent doing what *other* people wanted! The teenager admonished not to bring friends home or to reduce the volume of music might feel similarly. Nonetheless, an overriding impression of home is that it is 'not work', or 'not school'. We can relax, be ourselves. We do not have to put on a 'public face', we do what we want to do rather than what outsiders want us to do.

Some things, of course, *have* to be done in a home if it is to function properly: food to be cooked, the rooms to be kept clean, beds to be made, and so on. There is no doubt that 'housework' really *is* work, and that the energy used in doing it is the same as for many industrial or office jobs. If we are not to be completely selfish, we must modify doing what *we* want to take account of the fact that running a home takes effort. We have to put something in. It seems only fair that the effort involved should be shared in some way among the people

Figure 1.10

living in the home. We are moving away from the traditional view that members of a family have fixed roles. It is now much more common for men to share household chores, to help with the children, and to cook, and for women to go out to work.

In the same way as a more flexible approach has developed towards housework, so people living together at home have to adopt a tolerant and considerate attitude to the desire for all members of the household to 'do what they want'. Sometimes this can be very difficult. We can all recall incidents where different family members wanted to do things which would conflict. Often a compromise must be reached which partly satisfies all concerned. These sorts of situation may arise more often when there are big differences in the ages of the people at home. For instance, the elderly grandparents' desire for peace and quiet is not easily arranged when a new baby is also living in the house.

Q 8

Look at figure 1.10. How could the grandfather help in the smooth running of the home?

1.5
WHAT DO OUR HOMES MEAN TO US?

Almost all of us are born into and brought up within families living in homes. This close relationship we establish throughout our childhood means that we tend to have strong emotional ties with home, quite independent of the physical factors we have discussed. It is these emotional considerations which are perhaps the most powerful of all in establishing our feelings about home. In the final analysis, this bond between us and the other members of our family overrides the material considerations. When we become adults, maybe get married and have our own children, we set up a new 'home' within which the emotional links are forged again.

Not everyone will always be happy and well cared for in their own homes, and it is for this reason that alternative arrangements are sometimes made for children. The divorce of parents means that children live only with one parent rather than both, though they may see the other parent very often. A mother or father may die before the children are fully grown up, or they may be incapacitated in some way that makes it impossible for them to look after children. The state takes responsibility where it is necessary, and children can be looked after in 'homes' or are fostered in other families. In some societies, children of brothers and sisters are brought up together, sharing homes and parents, as well as grandparents and uncles and aunts.

Older people also need love and care from the people around them. In the United Kingdom, the population is an ageing one, and there are more and more old people who need to be looked after. If the state has to provide care it will cost a great deal of money; on the other hand, it is sometimes difficult for a family to look after its elderly members.

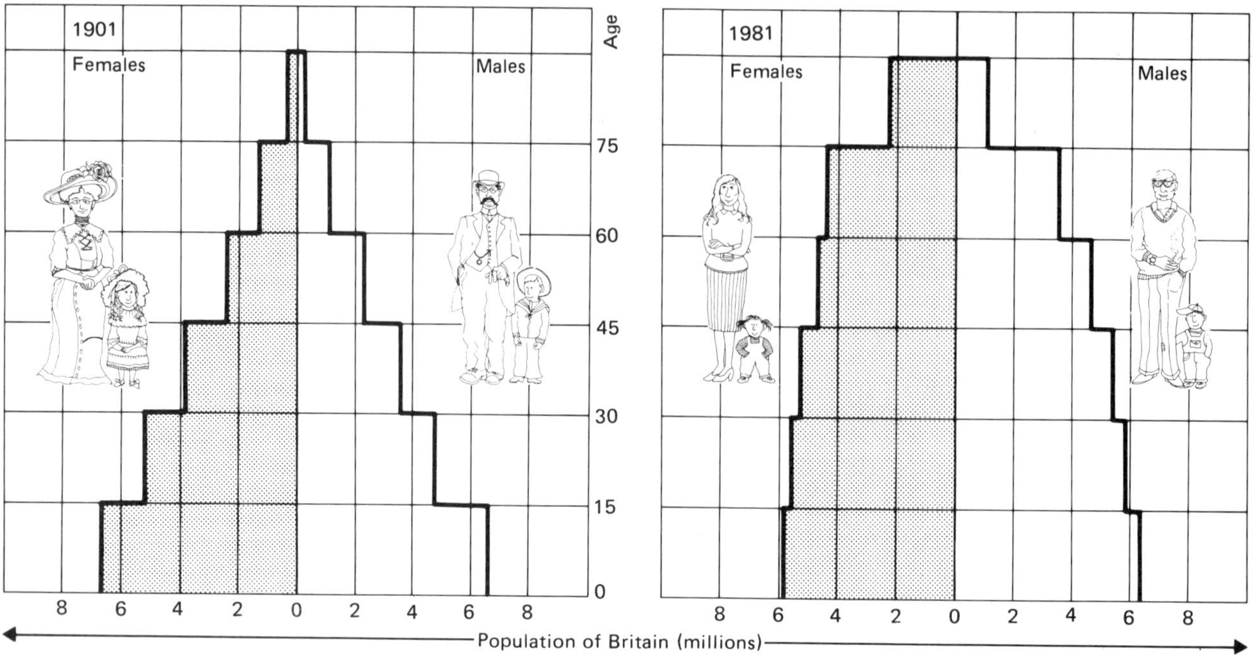

Figure 1.11
The numbers of people in different age groups in the population of Britain in 1901 and 1981.

Q 9
Look at the population statistics in figure 1.11.
a What are the most important differences in the population between 1901 and 1981?
b Why do we have an ageing population?

Q 10
What help is available to:
a families with old people
b families with babies and young children?

1.6 THE FAMILY WITHIN THE ENVIRONMENT

The home in which we live is part of a community. There are other people and places providing the things which we need to live comfortably. For thousands of years groups of people have lived closely together, providing between them the things they need for mutual support. For instance, medieval English villages had, among other things, a church, a baker, a shoe-maker, and a blacksmith. Heavy goods could not be transported for any distance until railways were built and roads were improved during the nineteenth century.

Nowadays, we can go much further than our immediate environment for the things we need, but nevertheless it is convenient to have some of them close at hand.

Q 11
Make a list of what you think is necessary for everyone to find within walking distance of their home. Using worksheet PM1, design a community to provide for the things you have listed.

BEING A HOUSE FATHER

For nearly twenty years John Burton has worked in and got to know many children's homes and institutions for people who need accommodation and help with everyday living. Since leaving his own home where he grew up (with his parents and sister) he has discovered that there are other ways of making a home, apart from the ordinary family one which he knew. Here is his account of what he thinks a home should be like.

For children, home is a place to grow up in, but for many reasons it may become impossible for them to stay with their own families. These children often have at least two homes which mean different things to them. One may simply mean the place where a child's mother or father lives, although it may only be one room and change frequently. Their alternative may be a large house shared with several other children and with paid staff whose job it is to make a home of it.

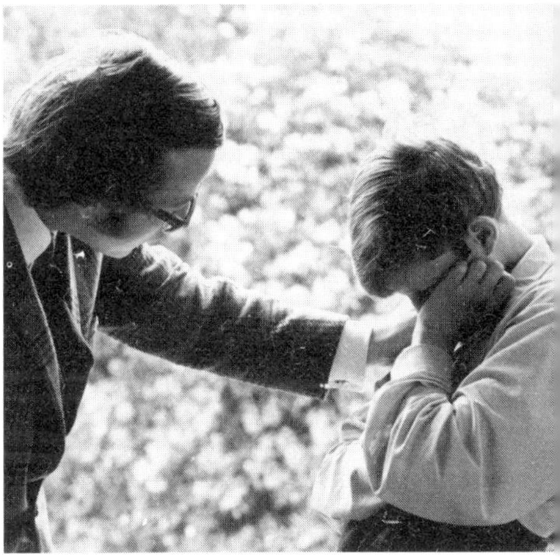

Figure 1.12
A house father at work.

Some children live in such a home for most of their childhood; others may stay for only a few weeks or months, but while they live there the place should be a real home to them. There are homes of different sizes and types: small homes with five or six workers and not many more children, homes for very handicapped children, homes specially for teenagers, and big homes with schools attached to them, but all of them need to be homely if they are going to help children to grow up happily and to become confident individuals. Having a room of your own or at least part of a room which is yours, choosing your own clothes, shopping and cooking, inviting your friends in, helping yourself to milk from the fridge when you come home from school and being welcomed by someone you trust, staying in bed late at the weekend: these are all details of everyday life which are specially important to children living away from their own families.

For some time now children's homes have officially been called community homes, and while that phrase rightly draws attention to their place in the outside social community, it can also refer to the inner community of a children's home. Often people think about the disadvantages of living 'in a home', but there can be many good things about it. Children who have spent some of their childhood 'in care' may be much better at getting on with other people, understanding them, caring for them, and living and working in a group in the future.

Residential social workers, the people who work in children's homes, need to believe in what they are doing and to like the children. It is a demanding job. All parents have to put up with their own children's naughtiness, moods, noisiness, getting into trouble, and learning to take control of their own lives. In a children's home too, the workers must be able to understand and tolerate the behaviour of other people's children and must create an environment in which children can make mistakes and and yet feel acceptance, care, and a sense of their own identity.

CHAPTER 2

A baby in the house

2.1
CHILDREN MEAN CHANGE

For new parents, the change from being a couple to being a family is an exciting prospect. With a baby, and children, there is always an extra person to consider and this may mean adapting to a life with less personal freedom, less money to spend as a couple, more responsibilities, and more fun.

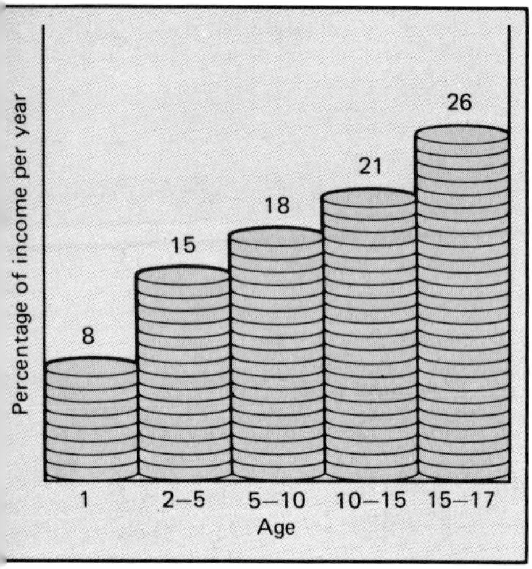

Figure 2.1
The percentage of an average couple's income which would be spent on one child each year.

Q 1

List some of the things that you think might be most worrying to the parents of a new baby. These might be worries about the baby himself – his or her health and whether they are caring for him in the right way – or worries about the changes they will have to make in their own lives, or money problems.

Figure 2.1 shows the cost of raising a first child to the age of seventeen.

Q 2

Why do you think a second baby might not cost so much?

MOTHER LOVE

A new mother may not immediately feel the maternal instinct she has been taught to expect. For many, 'mother love' is something that grows out of caring, with both mother and baby feeding back responses to the other so that a loving bond gradually develops between them. The infant cries, the mother comforts, so the infant stops crying and may even 'reward' the mother with a smile.

Figure 2.2
Mother love.

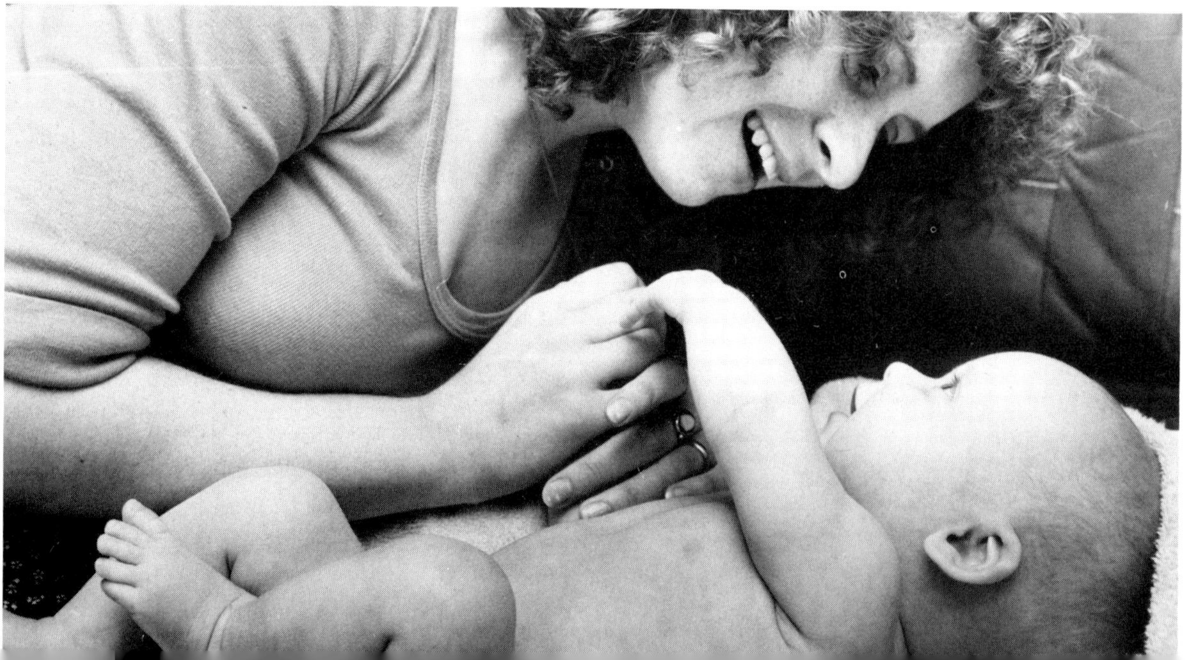

Q 3

a How can this 'reward' system sometimes break down?

b Do you think a mother is likely to feel differently about a baby who doesn't reward her in this way?

c What factors do you think can affect a woman's ability to love her child and care for it?

MOTHER SUBSTITUTES

Sometimes a mother goes back to work soon after her baby is born. Sometimes the father is able to stay at home to look after the baby. Often families have grandparents who are free to look after the young and in yet other cases a child-minder or nanny is needed.

Q 4

a What kinds of 'mother-substitute' care are available?

b Which do you think would be most satisfactory from the baby's point of view?

2.2

MEETING THE INFANT'S NEEDS

A new-born baby has very special needs, which he expresses by crying. The mother's job is to understand his needs and meet them. A baby will only demand what he actually needs at the time. For the first few weeks of life at any rate the baby's 'wants' are the same as his needs, and so the idea that you can 'spoil' a baby by 'giving into him' is a false one.

Q 5

List all the reasons you can think of which might make a baby cry. It may help you to do this if you can think of what you might do to make a baby stop crying.

BODY CONTACT

Picking up a baby to cuddle him will nearly always stop him crying. Close body contact is a real 'need'. Ideally, a baby would like to be carried around continually, but this could be very inconvenient.

Q 6

How can a mother fulfill her baby's need for close body contact? Other societies have recognized this need and found special ways of meeting it. What are they?

BREAST FEEDING

A baby's first need is for food and the food most readily available, clean, safe, and nutritious, is breast milk.

Q 7

List all the reasons you can think of why a mother should breast feed. Why might she need to bottle feed instead?

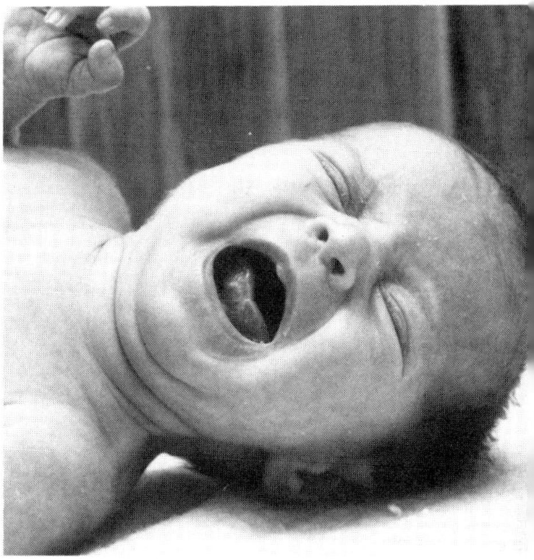

Figure 2.3
Why might a baby cry?

Figure 2.4
This baby feels secure and happy on its mother's back, while she has both hands free for working.

Figure 2.5

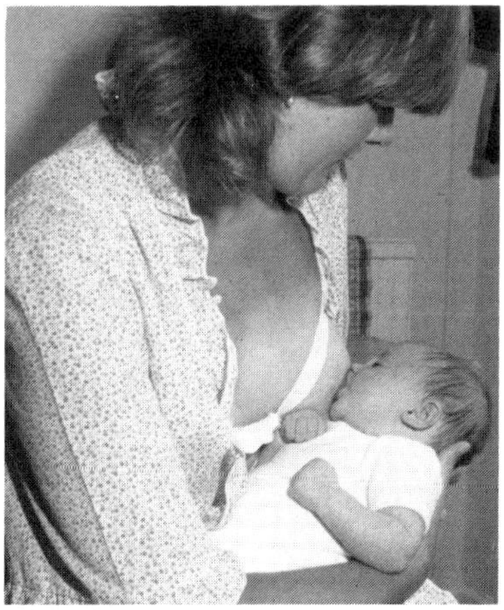

When you are answering this question you can consider how *safe* it is for the baby and how *convenient* each method is for the mother. You might also like to consider the *cost* of each method.

Breast milk is best for the baby. It is easy for him to digest and has exactly the right blend of nutrients. It also contains antibodies which protect the baby against disease. A mother's main worry about breast feeding is usually that she cannot see what the baby takes, and fears he may not get enough. The milk supply works on a supply and demand system — the more the baby takes, the more the breasts make. So if she thinks that her milk supply is low, feeding the baby more often will increase the supply. She should, however, be sure she continues with a sound diet herself (see *Nutrition*, Chapter 14).

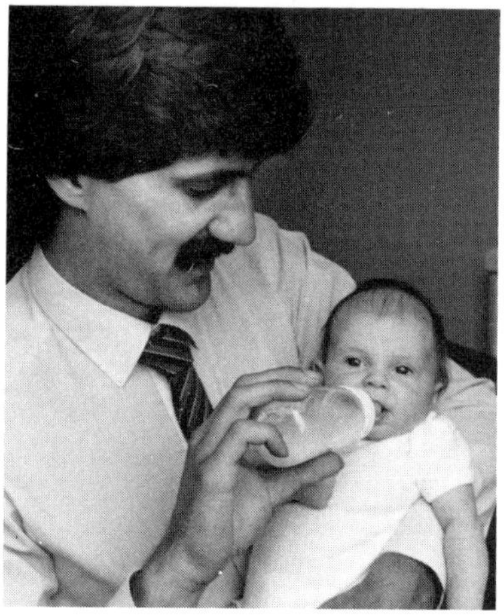

Figure 2.6

BOTTLE FEEDING

The mother who needs to bottle feed has four main points to remember if she is to make bottle-feeding as good a substitute for breast feeding as possible.

1 She must choose the right formula. A special baby milk must be used. The best baby milks have been modified to make them as much like human milk as possible. This also makes them the most expensive.

2 She must make up the formula exactly according to the directions given on the tin. The temptation is to give the baby too much — a level spoonful means just what it says. Level it off with a knife as shown in figure 2.7. If the solution is overconcentrated the baby's digestive system will suffer, and the baby will get too many calories and grow too fat. Habits established even as early as this may be difficult to change; fat babies often grow into fat adults.

3 She must be careful to sterilize all equipment — milk is an excellent breeding-ground for bacteria. Worksheet PM2 shows the daily routine necessary for safe sterilization.

4 She must make sure the baby gets as much cuddling and body contact with his feeds as the breast-fed baby — the baby should never simply be 'propped up' with a bottle. The fact that the father can bottle feed the baby too is one positive advantage of the method.

WEANING

The introduction of solid foods, and the gradual reduction of breast or bottle foods should begin when the child is about three months old. The baby can be offered a variety of foods. Some can be bought in cans and jars, but it is perfectly possible to liquidize or finely sieve the foods which the rest of the family are having. Salt and sugar should be kept to a minimum. (See *Nutrition*.)

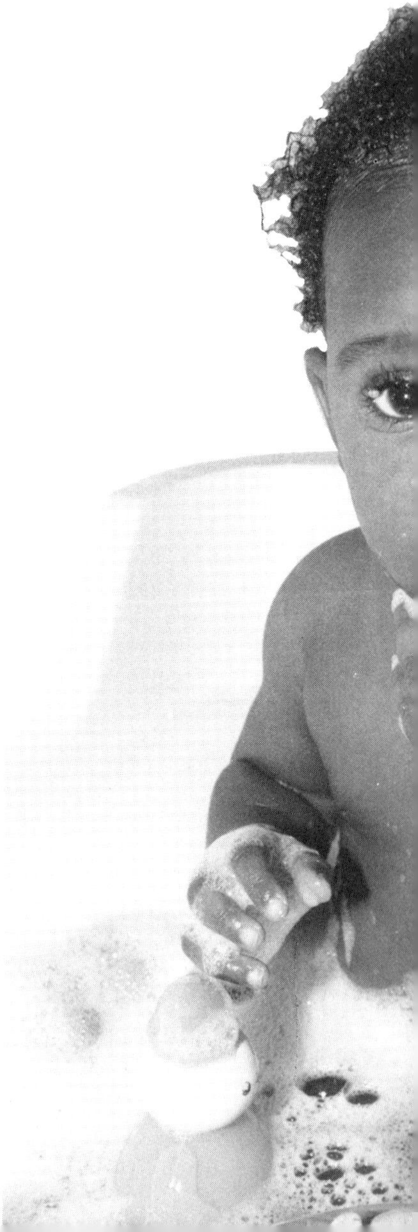

Figure 2.8

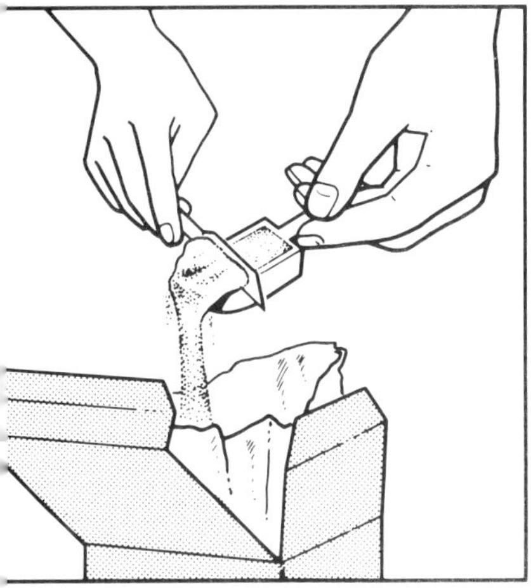

Figure 2.7

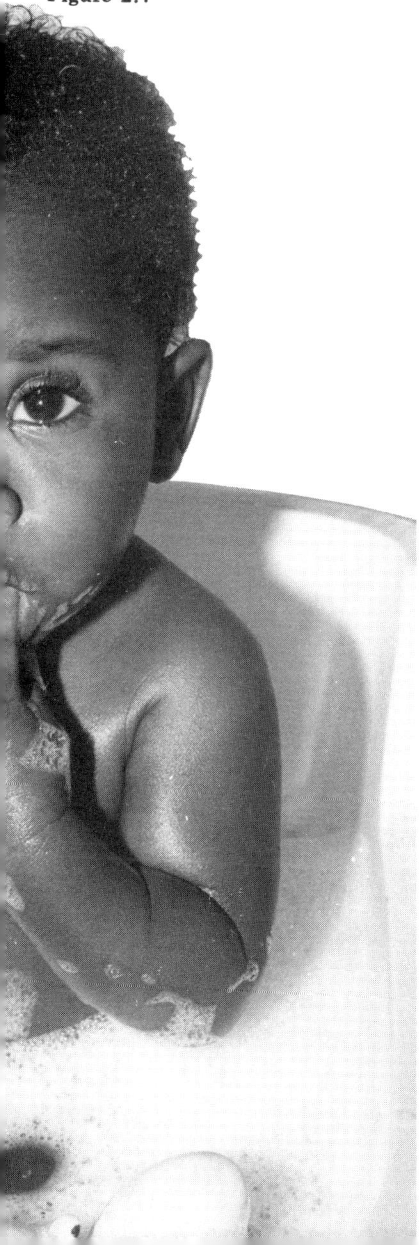

SLEEP

A baby will sleep just as much as he needs to sleep; parents of a new baby may suffer from lack of sleep; the baby never does. And so all the advice given to parents about helping the baby to sleep through the night is aimed at making life more comfortable for the *parents*, not for the child.

Q 8

Think about equipment and accommodation needed for a baby to sleep peacefully. What should the baby sleep in, for example, and should he share his parents' bedroom?

New babies can sleep anywhere; a padded box or drawer with a thick mattress will do as well as a traditional crib. It will help the baby to differentiate night from day if he is given a definite bedtime routine — perhaps a bath, a change into night-clothes, and a darkened room.

WARMTH

Babies lose heat quickly and easily. This is partly because they have a large surface area relative to their size from which to lose heat, and partly because the mechanisms which conserve heat in older children and adults do not work efficiently in infancy. A baby's room should be kept at around 20 °C to 21 °C, the room in which he is undressed and bathed should, however, be much warmer — about 29 °C (this temperature may feel rather warm to an adult).

Q 9

a How would you dress a baby to make sure he is kept warm enough?

b What other steps would you take to make sure the baby doesn't become dangerously chilled?

c Equally, how can you make sure the baby is not becoming overheated by wearing too much protective clothing?

CLEANLINESS

Q 10

How important do you think hygiene is in caring for infants? Do you think a daily bath is essential, for example? List what you think of as essential and non-essential in a baby's routine daily hygiene.

Some of a baby's equipment needs to be kept *sterile* — that is, all the bacteria must be killed. You have already seen that bottle-feeding equipment needs to be sterilized (see worksheet PM2) because milk is a good breeding ground for bacteria which might cause tummy-upsets. Nappies also need to be sterilized: bacteria will multiply in a dirty or wet nappy and might cause nappy-rash. The rest of his equipment — toys, rattles, plates, etc. — needs only to be kept *clean*. Bacteria will not grow on surfaces like wood and polythene and metal in any quantity.

The baby's face and bottom must be kept *clean* or they will become sore. But because the baby does not sweat and leads an inactive life there is no real need to give him a daily bath in the first few weeks.

A portable baby bath — or even a plastic washing-up bowl — which you can place at a convenient height in a warm room is the most convenient equipment, but a basin or sink will also do. When the baby is between three and six months you can start to use the big bath, provided that you use only a few inches of water and a rubber mat in the bottom to stop the baby slipping.

Babies may seem very fragile and slippery if you are not used to handling them, and so if it is not possible to have a class demonstration, you should try to watch a baby being bathed by someone else.

Bathing the baby

1 Undress the baby on a towel on your lap. Use the towel to wrap the baby in while you wash his face and head (with clean water, no soap, on the face).

2 Check the temperature of the water with your bare elbow. It should feel warm (not hot), *i.e.* about 37 °C.

3 Lower the baby into the water with your left arm behind the baby's head and your left hand grasping his shoulder. Your right hand should support his buttocks.

4 Withdraw your right hand to wash the baby's body (a baby bath liquid dissolved in the water is easier than soap.)

5 Lift the baby out, supporting him as before, and wrap him quickly in the towel.

Always test the temperature before putting the baby in and *never* add hot water when the baby is in the bath. ⚠
Never leave a baby or toddler alone in the bath or bathroom.

Q 11

List all the possible dangers of doing these things.

2.3
HOW DO CHILDREN GROW?

Babies and young children grow in both height and weight at a regular and predictable rate. The graph on worksheet PM3 shows the growth curves (obtained by plotting the baby's weight against his age in weeks) of boy and girl babies who were light, average, and heavy at birth. You can see that all these curves are the same shape, showing that the babies are all gaining weight at much the same rate.

Q 12

a What else does the graph show you?

b What would the graph look like if the baby was becoming much too fat?

Figure 2.9
Mealtimes can be battlefields . . .

DIET AND ATTITUDES TO FOOD

For many toddlers and parents, mealtimes are a battlefield rather than a pleasant social occasion. The right attitudes towards feeding are as important as the right food.

Q 13

Which of the following attitudes do you think are most likely to lead to trouble-free mealtimes as the child grows older, and which are likely to cause feeding problems:

a introducing the child to a wide variety of tastes and textures at an early age

b allowing him to 'play' with his food when he is learning to feed himself – picking it up in his fingers rather than eating it with a spoon

c making him eat everything on his plate

d accepting that he has likes and dislikes and adapting his diet to these

e withholding sweets, or giving them, as punishment or reward

f insisting on feeding him until he is old enough to feed himself properly and neatly

g refusing to allow a pudding unless and until he has eaten a first course?

Q 14

What do you think makes a bib, a high-chair, and a beaker necessary for a baby's mealtimes? Discuss this with your teacher.

2.4 MILESTONES

All children reach the 'milestones' of physical development in the same order — a child will not stand before he has learned to sit, for example. But the age at which a child masters each new physical skill can vary widely, by weeks or even months. So it is important not to compare one child's rate of development with that of another — it is 'normal' for a child to learn to walk at eleven months, and just as normal if he does not walk until he is eighteen months. If he is generally alert and responsive and active, it really does not matter if he has not reached a particular point of physical development at a particular time.

Keep a chart for at least a term — if possible for a full year — following a baby's development from birth. Record the ages at which the following milestones are reached:

first smile
raises head and shoulders from a face-down position
rolls over from face-down position onto back
first tooth
sits supported
sits unsupported
attempts to feed himself with spoon
crawls
pulls himself to standing
stands unsupported
takes unsupported steps.

Compare your results with those obtained by other members of the class. You will see what a wide variation there is. There is nothing parents can do to speed up the physical development,

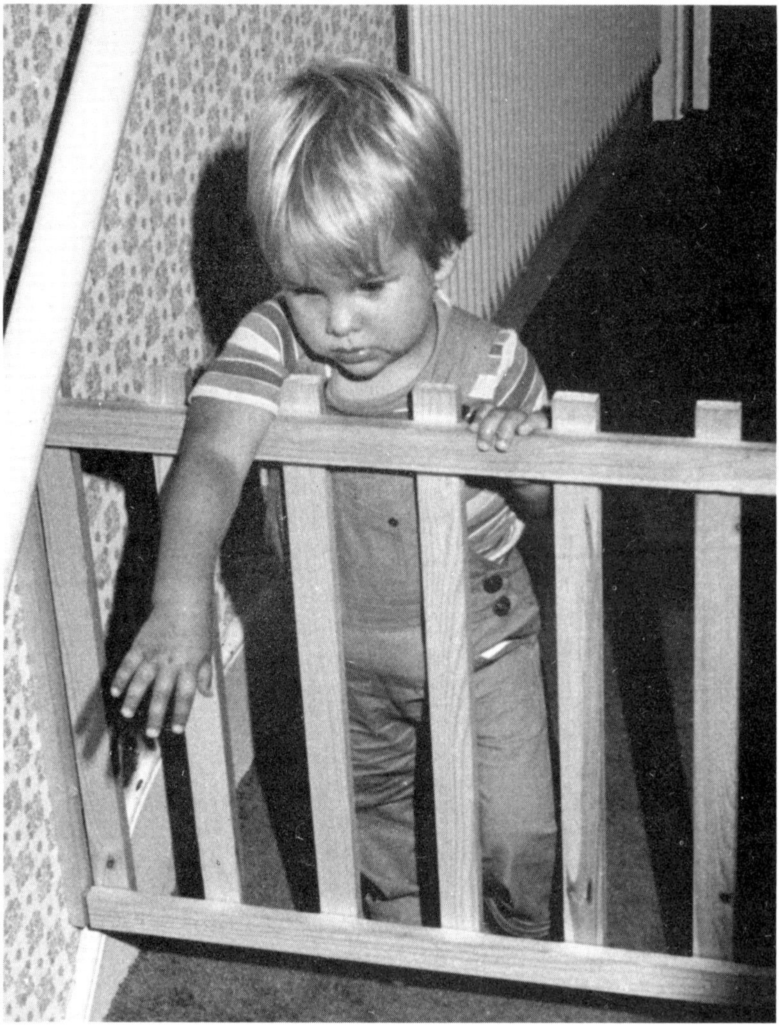

Figure 2.10
A safety gate is important.

and no advantage to them in doing so. (In Chapter 3 you will see that there are other areas of development in which parents can and should take a more active part in stimulating their children.)

Combine your results with those of the other members of the class to estimate the average age at which the children you have been studying reach these particular milestones. Does this correspond to the average age at which your teacher has told you that these milestones are usually reached?

2.5
ADAPTING YOUR HOUSE FOR THE MOBILE CHILD

An alarming number of accidents happen in the home and many involve children under the age of four (see Chapter 11). One of the difficulties of keeping a child safe is that you have always to be one jump ahead: the day you decide the child needs safety straps in his high-chair might be the day he will discover how to climb — and fall — out of it. The child has to explore the world around him because this is how he learns, but he lacks judgment, common sense, and forethought — all the qualities that keep an older person safe.

Q 15

What special dangers face a child of:

a six months
b crawling age
c toddling age?

Do window-shopping in two or three local stores (including, if you can a specialist store such as Mothercare) for a child's cot, a 'baby-bouncer' and a 'baby walker'. You need to think about *safety*, *performance*, and *price*. Notice that it is easy for manufacturers to make baby equipment eye-catchingly attractive. You may find examples of these or other articles which look so attractive that parents might not notice, or might be tempted to overlook, defects in their safety or performance.

2.6
TOILET TRAINING

Up to the age of about fifteen months a baby is not even aware of opening his bowels or urinating. The first sign of awareness comes when a child notices that he has made a puddle, or wet or dirtied himself. A few weeks later — usually towards the end of his second year — he will recognize the signs of a coming bowel movement; this is the stage at which he is ready to start using a pot. Bowel control is achieved before bladder control because there is a reasonably long interval between the 'feeling' and the 'action', long enough for a watching adult to help the child onto his pot. Bowel movements tend to be regular too, so that the parent knows when to expect them. It is much more difficult for a child to become dry; at first he will only recognize the sensation of impending urination when it is too late to control it. But by the age of about two he will learn to feel when his bladder is full and delay the flow for several minutes.

Some parents find that their babies are so 'regular' in their bowel movement that they can pot them 'successfully' from a very early age — a few weeks or months.

Q 16

What do you think are the advantages and disadvantages of this approach to toilet training?

If you can, find parents who use, or have used, this method and those who have practised the delayed training method discussed above. Try to find out, in each case, how long it took to 'train' the child, whether there was any difference in the age at which the child finally stopped wearing nappies because he was both clean and dry. It is best if you can talk to parents who have children at this stage or who have had recent experience of it. Parents of older children tend to forget the exact timing of events, or to remember them through rose-tinted spectacles and may claim to have been more successful than they actually were.

BACKGROUND READING

A CAREER IN CHILD CARE

Elaine Drummond looks after children for a living. Here is her account of her training and work.

During my last years at school I studied Home Economics and Biology, and in that time I decided I wanted to be a nanny. It is a worthwhile career if you have a great fondness for children, plenty of energy and lots of patience. Not only do we cope with children with happy smiles, but also with the tears and the tantrums. The term 'nanny' has rather an old-fashioned ring about it, but I like it. It suggests a warm and loving relationship with children which is a most important part of my work.

When I left school I decided to take a two-year full-time course, training in the care and development of children from birth to seven years of age. This equipped me to work with children within this age group and also with older children if I preferred, including nannying, day nurseries, nursery schools, hospitals and creches. My training involved both practical and theory work, and covered subjects such as the importance of play, and the physical, intellectual, emotional, social, and language development of children. It also included safety considerations, and developed my skills of observation.

Many mothers are choosing to return to work after having children and need someone to look after their children. Some people still want the nanny as a status symbol, but I have always tried to work with families where the mother is at work.

Figure 2.11
Elaine with a group of other nannies and children.

When you work as a nanny there are two alternatives. You can live with the family, but you can feel that you are imposing on the parents' privacy in the evenings and you can be made into an always available unpaid babysitter. It is also quite difficult to have a private life of your own. The alternative is to be a daily nanny where you travel to work and return home in the evenings. Being a nanny can be a lonely job as you are on your own during the day, but with a little effort you can make friends by joining groups for children, such as 'Mothers and toddlers' and 'One o'clock clubs'.

When you first meet your family it is very important right from the beginning to discuss all aspects of your job, including hours and time off, and any domestic work. I believe it is important to be in sole charge of the children, otherwise they do not know who to turn to and a lot of playing up against parents and nanny results. One of the nice things about being a nanny is that you sometimes get an opportunity to travel with the family, and you can find yourself visiting unusual and exotic places.

So far in my career I have been with one family for three years, and with my present families for just over one year. I look after two small boys both of whose mothers are at work. It is interesting to see the boys grow up together, but obviously it is hard work. In future I would like to spend some time working with children from families who may be going through difficult times. My training and experience should enable me to do this, and helping babies and toddlers to develop into happy and well-adjusted children is a very interesting and worthwhile career.

Figure 2.12
Elaine with her charges (Joseph and Barnaby).

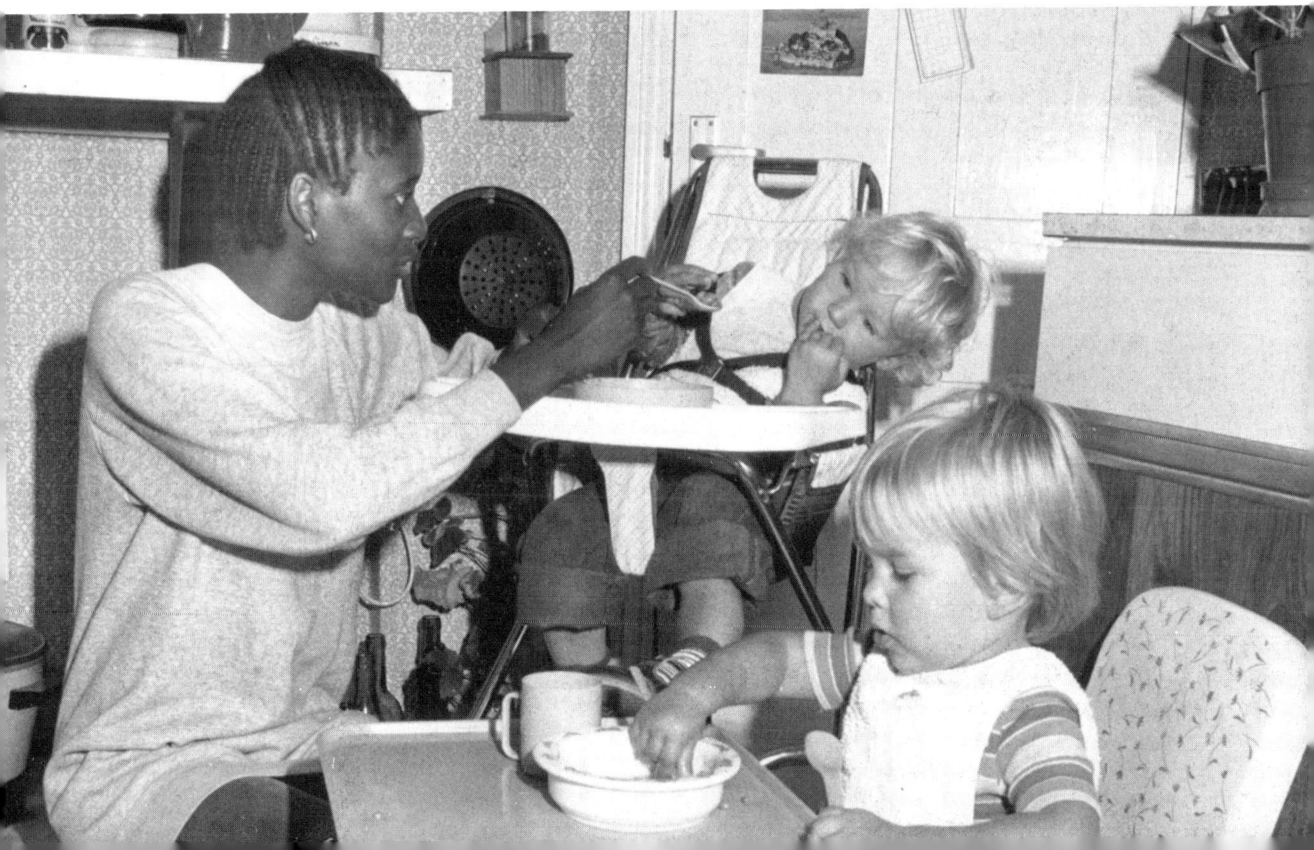

CHAPTER 3

Child development

3.1
LEARNING THROUGH PLAY

A child learns through watching other people and exploring everything around him. We call this 'play', but it is just as important to the child as any adult's 'work'. Almost everything is new and interesting to a child, and so almost anything can be a 'toy' for him.

Q 1

How do you think you can encourage a child to learn through play? Think about the things that most often affect the way *you* learn. What makes it particularly easy or difficult for you?

Here are some of the reasons why you might be discouraged from learning:

a Because you are bored. A person who stimulates your interest will be much easier to learn from.

b Because it seems too difficult for you. If you are continually frustrated because you cannot do something you may give up trying. Getting something right is a great spur to go on to the next step.

c Because no one has shown you how. You *can* learn to plane a piece of wood, or to understand French, by reading a book, but you will probably learn more easily, and do it much better, if you have watched or listened to someone who knows how to do it.

d Because you have been told the answer without working it out for yourself. This may seem easier, but does not actually teach you much.

Notice how important timing is. A toy or task that is too difficult may frustrate the child and make him give up trying. Something that is too familiar or easy may not arouse his interest enough to make him want to explore it any more.

Figure 3.1
Using household objects as toys.

Figure 3.2
Learning hand-eye co-ordination.

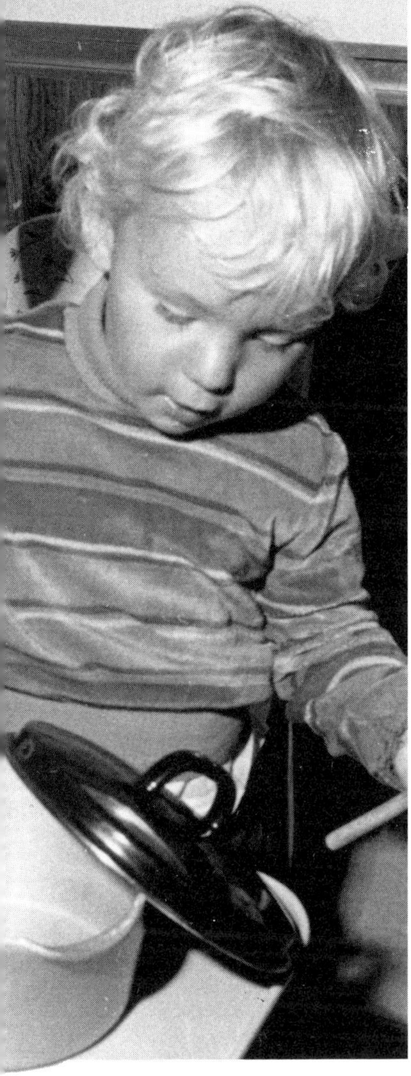

An important part is also played by the person who cares for the child. He or she is the child's 'model' — the child will listen and watch and imitate. They have to avoid the temptation to say 'let me do it' to a child who is working something out for himself, successfully if slowly, or to say 'you are not doing it the right way' when he is not doing it *their* way.

Think about the toys you believe would be the 'best buys' for a child. Remember that many household objects are potential 'toys'.

Spend some time watching children at a playgroup or nursery school. See which activities they spend most time on, which toys seem to get the most attention. How many of these toys and activities could you make or improvise? What would be worth saving up for because it would be so well used or difficult to make at home?

3.2 LEARNING HAND-EYE COORDINATION

When you hit or catch a ball you are using hand-eye coordination. Around two and a half to three months a baby starts to realize that his hands can affect the objects he sees — he can reach out for an object and if he manages to touch it the object will move. This is the beginning of hand-eye coordination. This is a skill the baby will learn in the end, but (unlike many other physical skills) it will develop faster if the baby is given the right kind of stimulation and plenty of opportunity to 'practise' this developing skill.

1 At six weeks babies simply like to look. They are very short-sighted and can only see clearly 25 to 30 cm from their faces.

2 At two to three months they will be able to hold something when it is put into their hands. They will start to watch their hands while playing with them and if they are shown something within reach, they will reach out and 'bat' it.

3 At three to four months they will try to judge the distance between their hands and an object, reaching out to try to grasp it. They may be frustrated now if they touch an object and it swings out of reach.

4 At four to six months they judge distances automatically and can reach straight out for the thing they want.

5 At seven to eight months they start to develop more complex movements, using fingers and thumbs separately. They will be able to push, to pull, to screw and unscrew, and to scribble with a crayon, if you show them how.

6 At ten months they learn to let go deliberately and drop whatever they are holding.

7 At one year babies can place things deliberately rather than simply releasing them and can throw things instead of just dropping them. They can oppose finger and thumb to pick up small objects too.

Q 2

a What toys would you provide for children at each of the ages mentioned above to help them develop hand-eye coordination?

b Apart from with their eyes, how else do babies explore the world?

3.3
LEARNING SPEECH AND LANGUAGE

All children go through the same stages in learning to speak. When the baby is about three months old, the cooing and gurgling of infancy gradually gives way to a more complex variety of sounds called 'babbling'. Babbling is the same for all babies, whatever their nationality or the language they will finally learn to speak. It is part of every baby's built-in programme of development. At first it is composed mostly of open vowel sounds, but gradually consonants are added, with 'm' being one of the first consonants to be acquired. In all languages the baby's first 'word' seems to be 'mama'; but this is in fact just a sound, not a word which will have any meaning for him until he is at least a year old.

From the age of about six months the baby's sound-making becomes more and more varied and elaborate. He will combine his various sounds and syllables towards the end of his first year and will sound so fluent and expressive that it will seem just as if he is talking a real, though foreign, language. At about this time, too, the child will start to use a particular sound (not necessarily the right one) to refer to a particular object. This is the beginning of true language — a sound is being used to communicate something specific to someone else.

Q 3

All babies babble, normally for the first six months or so of life. But a baby who is deaf will not go on to the next stage, to develop normal speech. Why do you think this is?

Anyone caring for a child has a very important part to play in helping him to develop speech and language. It is up to the adult to listen and understand and to talk to the child at every opportunity so that he is encouraged to go on talking. The first words are always 'labels' for things that are particularly interesting and important to him: a food he enjoys, shoes he is proud of, a favourite family pet. Talk to the child about what he can see around him. Use the proper words yourself, but don't correct him or pretend not to understand if he uses the wrong word, or one he has made up.

3.4
LEARNING ABOUT THE WORLD

Q 4

What kinds of play, and what kinds of toys, would you give to a child to teach him something about the 'real' world and its properties?

If you can, watch children at a playgroup using the sand and water corners. Watch them playing with dough too. (Dough is a good substitute for proper modelling clay, being easier to handle and less messy to use.) You will see them learning about the different ways solids and liquids behave — how sand will run as well as water but is not wet; how water can be carried in a beaker but not in a sieve; how dough can be moulded and keep its shape.

A sandpit and a paddling pool in a garden are ideal for this kind of play. But even in a small house or flat with no outdoor play-space, a deep tray or washing-up bowl of sand or water can be provided. Use the kitchen or bathroom, putting the tray or bowl on a protective plastic sheet, or even on newspapers. You will also need to protect the child with a plastic apron.

Figure 3.3

DRESSING UP

Children love to become someone else. Acting as people they have seen, or acting out situations that they may have experienced or been worried by is a large part of their play lives.

When things become a little difficult for them, it is a help for children to be able to control their emotions by acting them out in a secure situation where they know they cannot get hurt themselves or hurt someone else. Thus the child begins to learn to cope with the feelings of anger or frustration and the need for affection and love. Parents should observe their child at play because this may often explain the child's behaviour.

Q 5
Think of three situations which a child might be likely to act out. Why do you think he might choose these particular ones? Remember that the child knows that his pretend behaviour *is* pretend — he may allow himself to behave during a game in a way which he knows would be unacceptable in real life.

Children do not need elaborate costumes for their imaginative games, only a few simple props.

Q 6
Using only clothes and props you would be likely to find around the house or be able to improvise, how would you equip a child to be:

a a doctor
b a king or queen
c Superman or Superwoman?

Figure 3.4

3.5 LEARNING TO BE INDEPENDENT

A child can only learn to be independent when he feels secure. The toddler's determination is notorious — in fact, this stage is known to parents as 'the terrible twos'. Many of the difficulties arise because the child is struggling to become independent — he no longer wants to feel that anyone else has total control over his life, and will become frustrated and angry when such controls are imposed. But children still need to be protected and, however much they want to be independent, they can still feel frightened and retreat swiftly into babyhood if too much is expected of them, or when they run into difficulties. A child who suddenly becomes much more babyish and clinging than usual is probably worried or anxious about something. He will need more attention and protection, more hugging and cuddling until he feels secure again.

Much of the child's sense of security comes from having learned to know the world around him and being able to predict how the people in it will behave. If this stable, predictable world changes, the child is bound to feel worried and insecure.

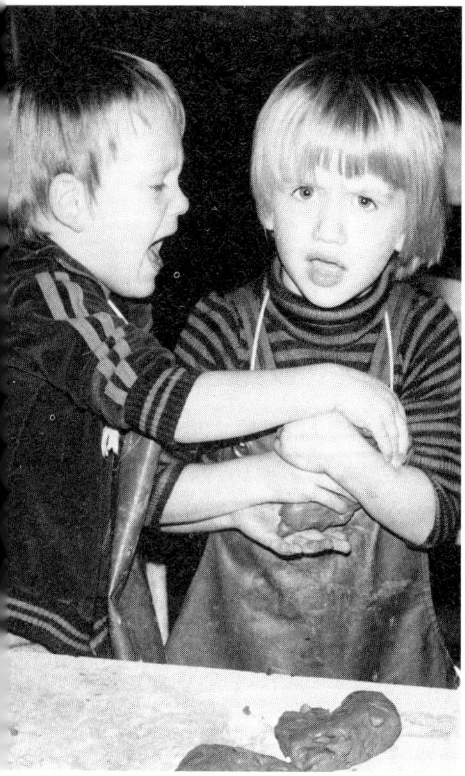

Figure 3.5

Figure 3.6
The expansion of a child's world.

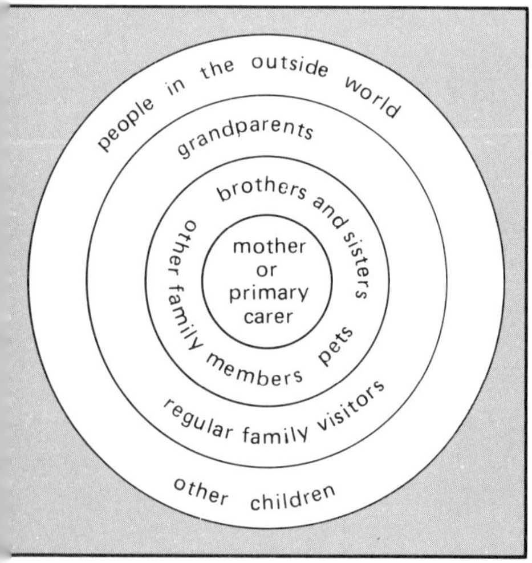

Q 7
What changes and events can you think of that may upset a child's world in this way?

REWARD AND PUNISHMENT
To encourage a child to behave in an acceptable way and to keep out of danger or trouble, clear guidelines must be given within which the child learns to behave and conform. The point is to teach the child to be able to control his *own* behaviour, which is increasingly important as he grows and becomes more independent from parental control. The use of punishment may be effective *at the time*, but the child will not learn any discipline from it, because the main feelings that it will produce in him are anger and resentment, rather than any understanding of why what he has done is wrong. Nor will he have any real wish to behave differently in future.

Q 8
How would you try to help a child of two to control his behaviour? Remember that you don't just want him not to behave badly – you want him to behave well.

The most common mistake that people make when they try to exert control is to concentrate only on the first of these two aims — preventing bad behaviour. So whereas a child's bad behaviour, or his potentially dangerous behaviour, may be punished, his good behaviour — the very things he does which you want to encourage — tends to be ignored. He may be given attention (which is probably the 'reward' he is seeking), when he is whining and behaving badly, for example, but earns no reward at all for playing quietly on his own. Reward good behaviour and don't reward bad is the first rule of good discipline.

The second is to make him understand why you are either asking him, or forbidding him, to do something.

The third most important rule is to remember that he will follow your example. The child who is routinely hit as a punishment, for example, will find it hard to understand why he is expected not to use violence towards another child.

3.6
LEARNING TO BE SOCIAL

The child's world gradually expands to include people other than the mother who is at first its centre. For the first year of life the baby is still very much dependent on his mother — or whoever is his 'primary carer' in the central circle (see figure 3.6). The baby will be anxious if he is separated from her or thrown into the company of strangers without her.

Toddlers enjoy playing alongside other children, but they are not yet ready to play with them. Ideas about 'sharing' or 'taking turns' are totally foreign to a very small child. By the time he is three or four years old the child is ready to learn this sort of social behaviour. It is then important that he has a group of friends of his own with whom to practise it. Pre-school children need companions of their own age with whom they can hold their own.

Q 9

By the time he is three or four years old, although not ready to be away from home all day, a child will probably benefit from some form of organized pre-school activity. What might a playgroup or nursery school be able to provide that a family might not?

3.7
THE CHILD AND THE FAMILY

Growing independence brings with it both freedom and responsibility for the child. He will be able to control more areas of his life, and make some important decisions for himself. You can start giving him control over small things very early — for instance, even a two-year-old can choose which T-shirt to wear, or decide whether to have honey or marmite on his tcast.

Q 10

Do you think that a child has 'rights'? If so, what are they? Discuss this with your teacher.

Think about the practical aspects of the child's life; for example, when and whether he should be allowed to choose his own clothes, or to choose his own friends. Which areas should parents control, and how absolutely should they control them? What do you think about pocket money — is it the child's by right or should he be expected to 'earn' it in some way? If he has a room of his own, should he be allowed at least a say in how it is decorated?

One of the things these questions probably indicated was how flexible parents have to be. Remember how long childhood seemed to you — the changes that took place seemed drawn out over an enormous length of time. You will have seen how much more quickly time goes by now. For adults, the changes in their childrens' lives take place so rapidly that it may be hard for them to adapt. Children's need for independence and the degree of control they are entitled to have over their own lives increase all the time.

Perhaps the other thing the questions showed was the variety of different attitudes held by people in the class. It would be surprising if there was general agreement on every question that was raised. Every child is part of a particular family, and will be brought up in that family's particular way, the way that suits them best. Some will find it easy to control their child, some will not. Some will attach great importance to manners and politeness, some to regular bedtimes and finishing up what is on their plate. Obviously, each family will concentrate most on

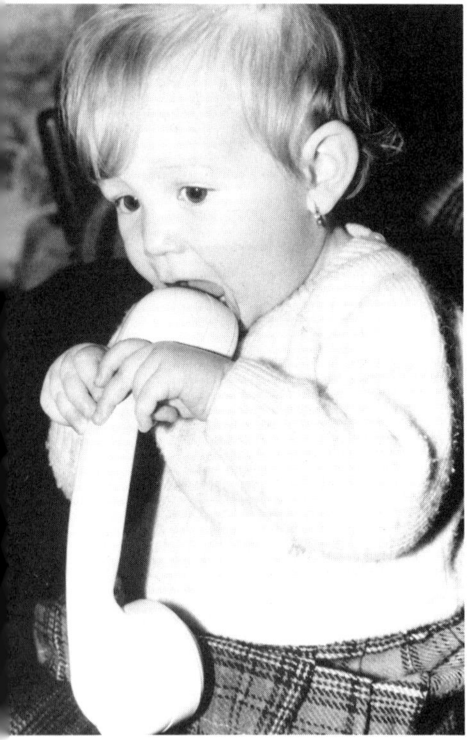

Figure 3.7
A telephone can be something to suck or bang on the table before the child realizes what it is and plays with it as a telephone.

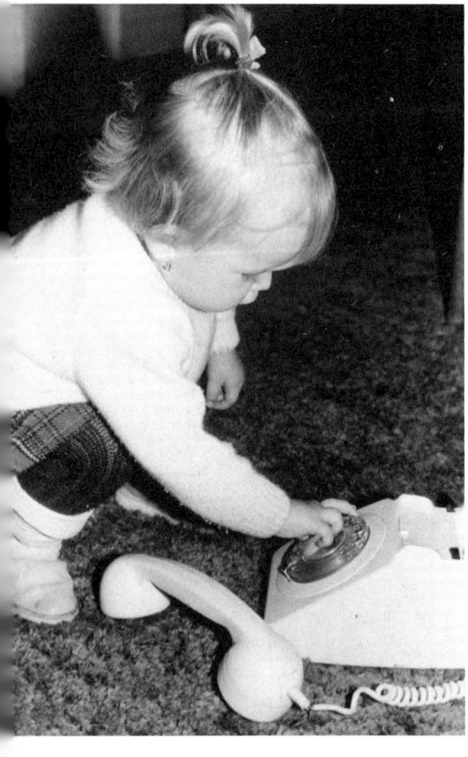

what matters most to them. But understanding what it is that *the child* needs may help them to compromise, if they can, on a style of upbringing that will meet his or her needs and yet not be too much at odds with the family's own inclinations or beliefs.

The last task, and perhaps the most difficult of all for the parent, is to accept that their child is a person in his own right, who may lack talents that they think important, or have others that may have never considered useful, or who may be able to find happiness in a way that had never occurred to them.

BACKGROUND READING

PLAYING WITH TOYS

Playing is very important for a child's development. She needs to learn to play with other people and with toys, and most importantly (and usually most fun too!) with both other people and toys together. The right toys help an adult to provide lots of positive attention and new ideas and encourage the child's emotional, social, intellectual, and physical development. They will help her to communicate with other people, to develop language, to think and act creatively, and to solve problems.

When choosing toys for a child you know well, think about what type of play they will encourage. For instance, telephones, musical instruments, books, and pictures encourage a child to communicate with someone else. Cars, teddies, dressing-up clothes, and dens make pretending easier. Rattles, posting-boxes, puzzles, and stacking beakers give practice in manipulating things with the hands. Balls, pull-along toys, tricycles, and climbing frames encourage agile movement of the whole body. Good toys are ones that children can do a lot of things with. Sometimes they can be played with differently as they grow older. They are not necessarily very expensive — the best are often home-made, everyday objects, or just people!

Attractive toys encourage adults to play with children at their own level. They can both be absorbed in a common task which makes the child feel that she is a person who can achieve things in her own right. Adults often enjoy playing with things like Lego or train sets just as much as children do, and may even take over and leave them out! You can encourage children who don't know you very well by playing with the toy yourself. Concentrate on the toys rather than the children and they will soon get interested and join in, and will not be nearly as shy as if you approached them directly. This is much more effective than trying to force them to play. Try to arrange the toys and activities in an order, starting with easy ones and ending with more difficult ones.

You can watch a child playing with toys in order to assess what she can and cannot do. Then you will know what she needs to learn or try out next. Perhaps try writing down what she does (sucking, twisting, building, throwing, and so on). When you choose her next toy, remember that you want to encourage what she is good at as well as practise what she has difficulty with.

CHAPTER 4

The world of young people

4.1
WHAT DOES IT MEAN TO BE A TEENAGER?

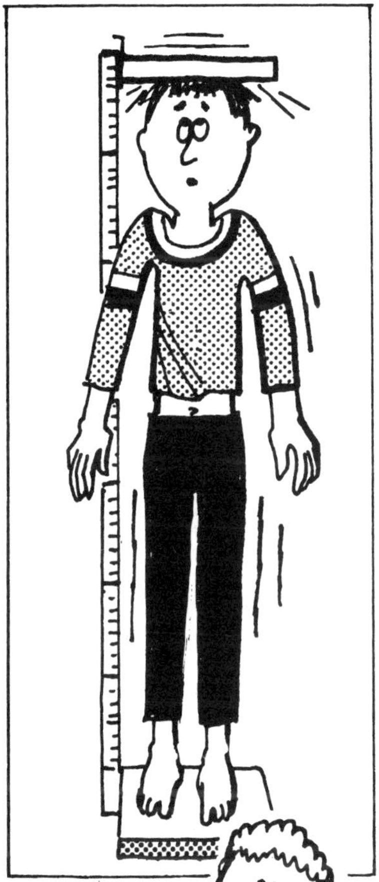

As you know, many changes take place during your teens. This can be described as a time of transition — that is, when you move from childhood towards becoming a more independent and self-financing adult.

1 Make a list of the changes that you think occur in your teens.

2 Examine your list to see whether the changes could be listed under common headings. For example, you might have written 'increase in height' or 'increase in weight'. These are clearly similar and could both be described as 'physical changes'.

3 Reorganize your list, grouping the changes under some common headings.

4 Now compare your list with those of everyone else in your class and combine the ideas to make a joint list. Make sure that you classify the changes under general headings, as in the example above.

5 Choose one of the changes on the composite list and, using reference materials, prepare a short talk presenting the facts about this topic to your class. Your talk should not last for more than five minutes. Use any visual aids that you think are relevant.

4.2
THE TEENAGER'S ROLE IN THE HOME

The many and varied changes occurring during your teens which you discussed in the last section can be thought of as changing your *role* (the part you play) in your family life at home.

Figure 4.1

Worksheets PM4 and PM5 contain *case studies* (examples) of situations that might crop up in everyday life. Read the case study that you are given and work through the questions on the sheet.

In the home, parents are increasingly aware that their children are becoming adults. However, some parents may find it difficult to adapt to these changes, and some teenagers may find that their parents still treat them as children.

Q 1
How can you encourage your parents to treat you as an adult?

4.3
HEALTH AND LEISURE

Throughout your years as a teenager you have to take more and more responsibility for your own health. Eating well (see *Nutrition*) will provide you with the nutrients and energy you need for living; exercise will prevent you from becoming sluggish and overweight; and plenty of sleep will give you vitality. How healthy you are is directly reflected in your appearance. Late nights, lack of exercise, snack foods, and missed meals will all result in a poor complexion, dull hair, and a general absence of sparkle.

Ideally, leisure time should be spent doing something practical and active, as well as talking to friends, or listening to music, watching the television, or reading a book or magazines. Living at home with your family means that everyone should consider everyone else in the household; playing a radio very loudly, for example, can disturb others.

Q 2
What opportunities exist in your own life for leisure pursuits out of school or college? Are you making the most of them?

Q 3
How would you like to spend a summer holiday weekend?
Draw up a schedule. Here are some things to think about.
a What part does your family play in your scheme?
b What clothes and equipment will you need?
c What food will you eat?
d Are your chosen activities healthy and safe? If not, what are the risks and are they worth it?
e What arrangements are necessary before leaving an empty home?
f Try to assess the cost to your family.
g Of course, you may find that your ideas involve spending more money than you or your family can afford. Go back over your plans and see how they can be adapted to a very restricted budget.

Some activities in which young people take part can severely damage their health. There are many accounts in the newspapers of the tragic effects of drugs, solvent sniffing, and excess alcohol.

Q 4
What are the dangers of these habits? How would you avoid being persuaded by someone you know to take a drug or sniff glue?

Figure 4.2

Figure 4.3

4.4
THE TEENAGER'S ROLE IN SOCIETY

As you go through your teens, your role in society is affected by the law. Your new legal rights bring both privileges and responsibilities. For example, the law permits you to drive a moped at the age of sixteen, and a motor-bike and a car at the age of seventeen. You can buy cigarettes at sixteen and an alcoholic drink at eighteen. When you reach the age of eighteen you have the right to vote in a general election, and to serve as a member of a jury. With these rights go the responsibilities to drive with care and skill, to exercise your democratic right to vote, and to take your place as a fair-minded member of a jury. You will no longer be able to travel at child fares or go into cinemas and theatres without paying adult entrance fees.

These changes in your legal status make you feel that you are now an adult. You can also expect to be judged and treated as an adult in your relations with society.

Q 5

Discuss the advantages and disadvantages of reaching adult status.

4.5
TEENAGERS AS CONSUMERS: WHY DO YOU BUY THINGS?

Chapter 14 looks more generally at the 'consumer society', and you may find it useful to read through it now. In this chapter you are being asked to consider some of the problems you may encounter now, particularly when planning how to spend your pocket money or money you have earned at a Saturday or holiday job.

It is often said that young people nowadays have more choices than ever before. Many of the problems that you face now in deciding what to buy are even more important when applied to all the choosing and buying that you will do when you have more money and responsibilities. But if you learn to make good decisions at this stage and to choose wisely the things you need now, this will help you later on.

It is also said that there are many 'external influences' which may affect teenagers.

Q 6

a What do you think is meant by 'external influences'?

b Do you think you are affected by them? Discuss the reasons for your answer.

One of the 'external influences' liable to affect teenagers is advertising. Advertisements are often aimed at teenagers because they are considered to be a group of people with a high *disposable income* compared with other age groups. Disposable income is the money that people have available for spending after they have paid for all of their basic needs (in other words, after they have paid the bills for rent or mortgage, essential food and clothing, and so on). So it could be called 'spending money'. As teen-

Figure 4.4

agers seldom have bills to pay, but often receive pocket money or payment for weekend or holiday jobs, they are said to have relatively high available spending money.

The advertisers hope that teenagers will be influenced by their advertising and *motivated* (or persuaded) to purchase (or consume) their product. Advertisers also believe that teenagers may affect family decisions about what to buy. Teenagers' opinions are thought to influence the choice of goods that families buy. Thus advertisers hope to persuade teenagers that they should not only buy goods for themselves, but also motivate their parents and other members of the family to buy goods.

Q 7
How do you think this might happen?

Advertisements on television can be particularly powerful. The images are zoomed directly into your home. They are very attractive and very expensive to produce and broadcast. Find out more about advertising on television for yourself.

YOU WILL NEED:
Access to a television

1 Watch the advertisements shown on one of the commercial stations for the following periods of time: one hour in the morning; one hour in the afternoon; and one hour in the evening.

2 Do this on a weekday and at a weekend.

3 Keep a record at all times of the following information: the day of the week; the time of day; the types of products advertised; the brand names of the products advertised; the number of times that the advertisements appear; which advertisements you think were aimed at teenagers. Add a short description of the style of advertisement, such as 'lively, musical, boy meets girl', etc.

Q 8
What percentage of advertisements do you think were aimed at teenagers?

Q 9
Which products were most often advertised to teenagers? Make a list.

4 Conduct a 'consumer survey' in your class. Find out the number of people who buy each of the products on your list.

Q 10
Do you think that the advertisements are successful as far as your class is concerned, that is, do they achieve their main aim – to sell the product?

BACKGROUND READING

LESSONS FOR THE FUTURE

Pick up a history textbook on Britain in the twentieth century and you will find the word 'recession'. 'Britain between the wars experienced a recession.' There was widespread unemployment, poverty, malnutrition, and misery. The recession did end; but did people alive then know it would end? As you live through the years of your teens, it is impossible to know how the period will fit into the time before or afterwards. For example, some people think that the last quarter of the twentieth century will one day be called the Third Industrial Revolution. Others see it as a period of recession, high unemployment, and social unrest. We can't know what will happen next.

In the early 1980s, unemployment rose to levels not seen since the 1930s. Economists described a combination of high 'cyclical' unemployment with high 'structural' unemployment. Cyclical unemployment is due to short term changes in the levels of industry's sales. Structural unemployment is the result of the long term decline of one or more major industries. Those out of work due to short term changes usually find work more easily than those whose industry is in decline.

Is it important that you have a job? We are a very job-orientated society. Some of the reasons that people go to work include: money, job satisfaction, convention, making friends, and a sense of 'identity' or 'vocation'.

Being without a job affects different people in different ways. A middle-aged man who is made redundant might have a mortgage to pay off and a wife and children to look after. It may be difficult for him to find a job as good as his old one. An unemployed teenager may not have as many problems as this, but knowing that someone is worse off than you never makes things any easier. Being young and unemployed can mean boredom, lack of self-esteem, and lack of money.

Unemployment *can* mean other things too. It can give the freedom and flexibility to take a course, learn a skill, keep fit, or do voluntary work. It can allow time to discover what a person really wants to do in life. People can take on part-time work, job share, or start a business.

In the future people are going to spend more and more of their lives learning. As new technologies come into use people have to be trained to use them. Someone starting work now may retrain several times during their working life. People now in their seventies and eighties have seen great changes in their lifetimes (ask them!); there is every reason to think that teenagers today will see changes that are just as great.

Figure 4.5

CHAPTER 5

Households with special needs

5.1
WHAT MAKES A HOUSEHOLD?

The people who have been described so far in this book have tended to live together in groups or families. But not everyone does live as part of a group. In fact, an increasing number of people live alone in what is known as a *one-person household* or a *single-person household*.

A household is officially defined as 'any group of persons, whether related or not, who live together and share housekeeping expenses', or 'any person who lives alone and is responsible for his or her own meals'. So a household is a unit of people and not, as it is sometimes described, a house, or flat, or any other place where people live.

People living in groups can help one another; for instance, a family may care for one of its members who is physically or mentally handicapped, or merely old. However, when such people live alone their special needs may require special help from the community at large. In addition, grants may be available to pay for things like extra heating in very cold weather.

Members of a household do not need to be related to each other, and the household can contain any number of people from one upwards. A household is known as a one-person or single-person household if it comprises one person, a two-person household if it comprises two persons, and so on, according to the number of people in it.

5.2
RECENT CHANGES IN HOUSEHOLD SIZE

A number of social changes have taken place in the United Kingdom in the last thirty years. These have meant that the average household size has become smaller — people are now living in smaller groups.

Q 1
What is meant by the phrase 'average household size'?

How is it known that the average household size has fallen? The evidence for this statement can be found in the results of two social surveys which the Government carries out each year. These surveys are called: the Family Expenditure Survey (or FES), and the General Household Survey (or GHS).

Figure 5.1
Living alone.

Frequency table

Household size	Number of households
1	1306
2	3654
3	3214
4	2530
5 or more	1707
Total	12911

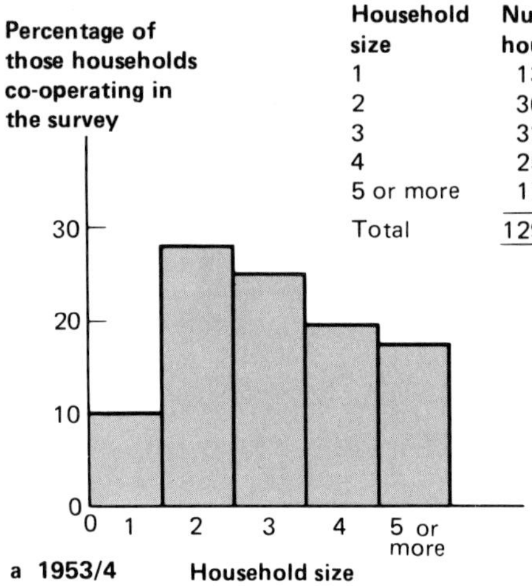

a 1953/4

Frequency table

Household size	Number of households
1	1556
2	2432
3	1265
4	1429
5 or more	243
Total	7525

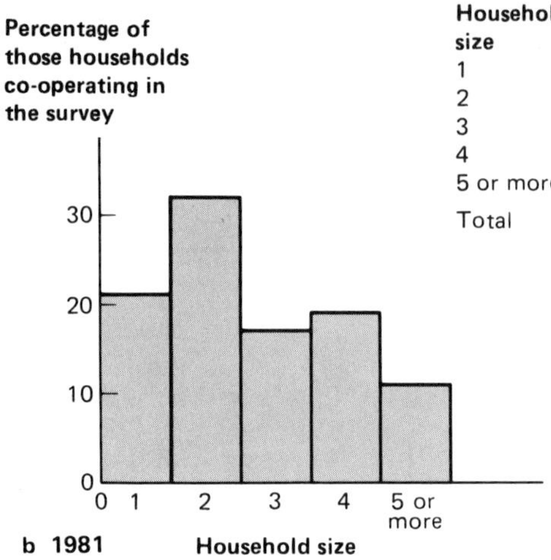

b 1981

Figure 5.2
The distribution of households by household size in 1953/4 and 1981.

The surveys are conducted to find out what changes are taking place in the ways in which people live and spend their money. People in households selected at random from the population are asked certain questions, including one about the size of the household in which they live. The FES, which has been carried out each year since 1953/54, has included this question each time. The data collected since 1953/54 is used to study changes in the size of the groups or households in which people live.

The bar charts in figure 5.2 show the distribution (or spread) of different household sizes in 1953/54 and in 1981.

Q 2
Examine the bar charts in figure 5.2 and answer the following questions in two parts, first for 1953/54 and then for 1981.
a Which household size is most common?
b What percentage of all households are one-person households?
c What percentage of all households are two-person households?
d Calculate the average (or *mean*) household size. Use this formula:

$$\text{mean household size} = \frac{\text{total number of people}}{\text{total number of households}}$$

Q 3
a What changes have there been in the percentage of households with 3, 4, or 5 members since 1953/54?
b What changes have there been in the percentage of households containing 1 or 2 people since 1953/54?
c What overall change has occurred?
d What social reasons can you suggest for these changes?

Q 4
How many people are there in your household?

Does everyone in your class live in the same size household?

Q 5
a Conduct your own small survey of household sizes among the members

of your class and record the results in the same way as figure 5.2.
b Which household size is most common among the members of your class?
c How many of you live alone in a single-person household? Does this surprise you? Why?

Q 6
Calculate the mean household size for the class.

Q 7
Now compare the findings from your small survey with the findings of the FES for 1981 shown in figure 5.2. What are the similarities and differences between these two groups of findings? Discuss the reasons for these.

5.3
WHO LIVES ALONE?

In section 5.2 you saw that there has been a rise in the number of people living alone. Now find out who they are.

Q 8
a Do you think it is an invasion of other people's privacy to try and find out who lives alone?
b Why do you think the Government should want to know who lives alone and what type of people they are?

Q 9
How many people do you know who live alone? Discuss with the other members of your class the type of people whom you know do live alone. Do they fall into any particular age group? What sex are they? Do they have any special characteristics?

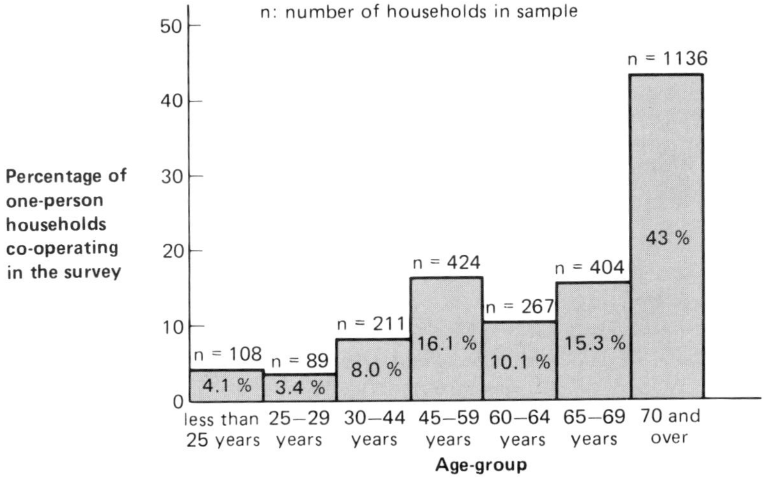

Figure 5.3
The distribution of one-person households by age-group.

Q 10
Look at figure 5.3.
a To which age group do the majority of people who live alone belong?
b What percentage of people living alone are over 60 years old?
c What percentage of people living alone are under 60 years old?
d Which age group in the under 60-year-olds contains the most single-person households?

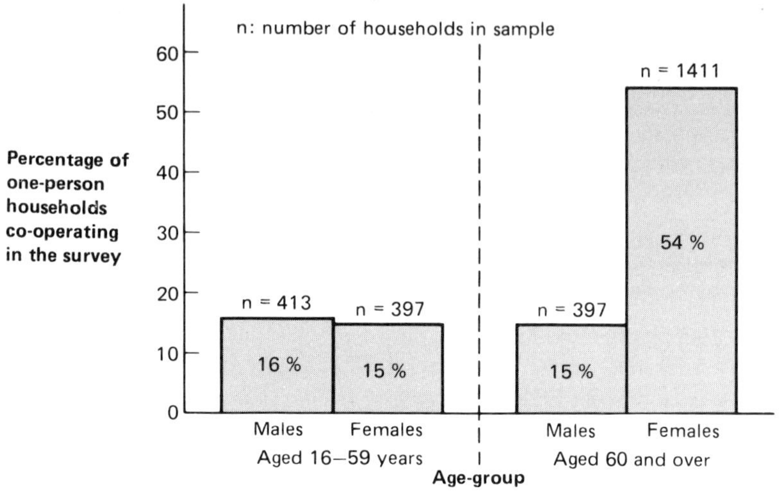

Figure 5.4
The distribution of one-person households by age and sex.

Q 11
Now look figure 5.4.
a What is the sex and age group of the people who form the largest group of single-person households?
b What is the difference between the percentage of males and the percentage of females living alone who are aged between 15 and 59?
c What is the difference between the percentage of males and the percentage of females living alone who are over the age of 60?

Q 12
Explain the reasons for the statistics shown in figures 5.3 and 5.4.

WHAT DO YOU NEED TO LIVE ALONE?

Having identified the groups of people who live alone, you should now be able to discuss their housing needs.

Q 13
What differences are there between the needs of people who live in single- and multiple-person households?

It may help to think of the activities conducted in the home for which different spaces may be required, and of the ways in which housing meets our emotional needs, and to remember that these are needs which are common to all.

5.4
SINGLE-PERSON HOUSEHOLDS WITH SPECIAL NEEDS

In figure 5.4 all single-person households are divided into four groups according to sex and age group.

Q 14
Which of these groups will have special needs? List these special needs and identify the groups to which they apply.

What housing, if any, is available in your local community for these groups of single-person households who have special needs?

What can you do to find out?

1 First you should use any references available in your school or public library, your home economics room, and your own home (*e.g.* newspapers) to find out what types of housing are recommended for single-person households with special needs.

2 Then you should contact local agencies, such as the Citizens Advice Bureau and the Housing Department at the local District Council Offices, to see whether any special single-person housing is provided locally. If it is, then find out exactly what it comprises. You should consider number and size of rooms, special facilities, location, age, style, and overall size.

What is the demand for this housing?
What is the cost to the individual?
How many available units are there?

3 Ask questions such as these until you have a clear description of the housing provided, how many people need this housing, and how much of this type of housing is available locally. (For the last details you may find that the local Housing Department can only give you an estimate.)

Q 15
Write down a detailed description of the type of special housing provided for single-person households in your neighbourhood.

Q 16
How well does this housing meet the special needs of the group(s) that you identified in question 14?

Q 17
Does the amount of special single-person housing provided in your neighbourhood match the estimated number of local people requiring such accommodation?

Discuss your answers to questions 14 to 17 with the other members of your class.

5.5 OTHER HOUSEHOLDS WITH SPECIAL NEEDS

Obviously, many elderly and disabled people live with their families rather than by themselves or in institutions.

Q 18
Imagine that you had had an accident and were disabled, even only temporarily. How would you and your family have to adapt to this? What alterations might need to be made to the house?

Q 19
What are the advantages and disadvantages of having a grandparent living with some of his or her family
a to grandparent
b to the family?

Some household equipment is difficult for elderly people to use. Look at some of this for yourself.

YOU WILL NEED:

Screw-top pill bottles (ordinary and child-proof)
Heavy cast-iron saucepan
Tin openers (various different types)
Packets of biscuits in plastic and paper wrappers
Left-handed potato peeler
Screw-top jam jar or similar
Milk carton

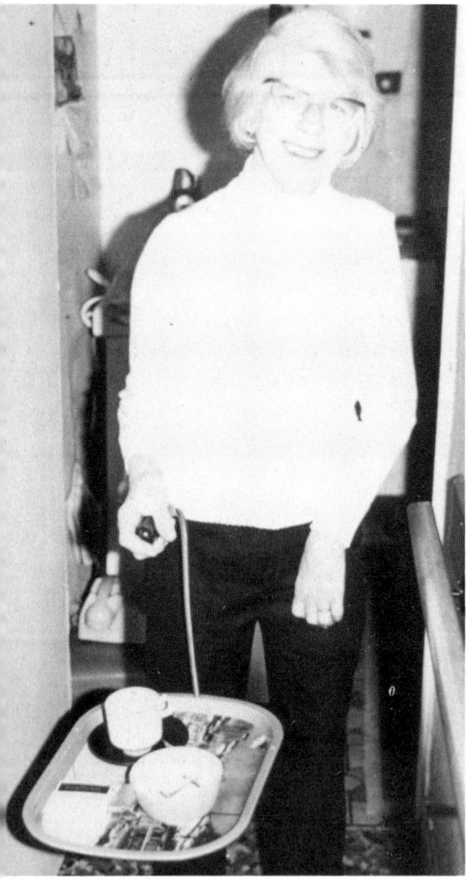

Figure 5.5
Encouraging independence: a tray for people who have had a stroke and can only use one hand, and a jar opener for people who cannot use their hands very well.

1 Assess each piece of equipment as being easy to use for
a an old person
b a person who is disabled and unable to use their hands easily.

2 In each case, suggest an alternative or explain what might make each item easier to use.

BACKGROUND READING

DISABLED, NOT UNABLE

My name is John Stewart and I am paraplegic (paralysed from the waist down) and so confined to a wheelchair. Despite this drawback, I maintain a full-time job as lecturer in the Polytechnic of North London. I live some distance from London (near Southend), but I commute successfully on British Rail when I am required in college, which is quite often in the week.

There are two alternatives for people in my position: either you adapt the home you already live in, or you choose a home which is already reasonably suitable. After hard searching, I eventually found a house that needed very little adaptation. (I had been living on a barge on the River Thames before my accident, to which I would now readily return, but at first I had neither the confidence nor the determination.) The modifications to my chalet bungalow are therefore minimal — a ramped path to the back door and two hoists.

The most significant need I have is a little assistance. I can exist effectively alone, but after a hard day at work, from which I frequently do not return until 9.30 pm, it is good to know that there is someone to meet me and prepare any cooking I require. I have been very well served by people from Community Service Volunteers and a scheme organized by the Department of Education and Science, but there are many others with my undemanding needs. The more volunteers that people like me can attract, the greater the possibility of our contributing to the society in which we live.

Now to the photographs of me in my Levo chair (figure 5.6). In one you can see me in my customary position, where my height is 4 feet and 8 inches. In the other I am standing to my full height of 6 feet. This is not merely of psychological benefit, it also allows me to work more effectively — reaching books on high shelves, writing on the board, and so on — which is why the Manpower Services Commission supplied me with the device.

I am disabled, not handicapped, but there are several sources of handicap to me. I cannot climb up stairs — but who wants to if he can travel by lift or be carried? I can't dance — with the present state of dancing I don't think I am missing very much! (My attitude to wheelchair dancing it is scarcely appropriate for me to express here.) I don't wear out shoe leather, and that is scarcely a disadvantage.

A factor which is sometimes a disadvantage is the attitude of society, and this is an aspect in which you can be influential. Remember that a disabled person may not be handicapped, he may be as able as you or more able than you. If you maintain this attitude, you will be providing us with what we seek, acceptance.

Figure 5.6
a *John Stewart in his wheelchair.*
b *This new Levo chair enables him to 'stand up' for the first time in fourteen years!*

a

b

CHAPTER 6

Finding somewhere to live

6.1
A CHANGE OF SCENE

While you are still at school you probably live at home. The meaning of the word 'home' and all that you understand by it was discussed in Chapter 1 of this book. When you leave school you may have to consider where you will be living.

Q 1

Discuss where you might live in the following situations:

a working in a local office or factory
b going to college or university
c following a course at a local technical college
d working in a large city.

Q 2

In which of the situations listed above are you most likely to have to be independent of your present 'home' situation?

Q 3

What might it mean to be independent? List the things about which you would have to make decisions if you were living away from home – for example, planning and preparing meals; working out how to allocate your wage/salary; washing and cleaning your clothes.

Figure 6.1
Independence has its problems.

6.2
WHERE TO LIVE

If you are moving away from home to work or study you will have to find somewhere to live.

Figure 6.2
Organize your time!

Q 4

a Draw up a list of factors which you will have to consider in deciding what to look for. For example, these might include the location of work/college, the available transport, the time it will take to travel to and from, the availability of cheap accommodation.

b Discuss the relative importance of each of these factors with the rest of your class.

c Imagine that you are moving into the nearest large city to begin working, with some 'day release' to continue your training at a technical college. Use the information available locally to decide on where you might live and explain what has helped you to make the decision.

6.3
PAYING YOUR WAY

In section 6.1 you listed things about which you might have to make decisions if you were living away from home.

Q 5

a Using this list, discuss as a group and agree upon a list of expenditure, putting it under two headings – essential and non-essential.

b Look at the list of essentials. Could it be subdivided under further headings such as food, shelter, and clothing?

c Try to make contact with a variety of people who are prepared to discuss with you in general terms the allocation of their income. Some people do not want to talk about money matters as they consider this a private matter. You might find that students, newly married young couples, or your own family would be prepared to discuss the subject with you.

d From these discussions, make a rough estimate of what percentage of your income you might have to allocate under the headings of food, shelter, and clothing.

e Make suggestions as to what you would do with the balance of your income. Illustrate your answer using a pie chart or a bar chart.

In addition to the basic rent, there will be other expenses involved in the provision of 'shelter' for yourself.

Q 6

Refer back to your notes about the people with whom you discussed allocation of income. Did they list any other expenditure connected with providing shelter? After discussion with your group make a list upon which you can all agree.

You will probably have included the following in your list:

house rates
water rates
insurance
gas/electricity accounts
(and perhaps telephone).

Q 7

a You will now be able to work out a more detailed analysis of how the percentage of your income which has been allocated to 'shelter' would be spent. As a group, discuss your findings and agree on the percentage of total expenditure for each item on your list. Assume that you are

just moving away from home and there is only yourself to consider.
b Construct a pie chart or bar chart to illustrate your answer.

6.4
WHAT IS AVAILABLE?

Having decided what percentage of your income to allocate to 'shelter', you are now in a position to investigate the types of accommodation which might be available. Do this following the assumption made in section 6.2 (that is, moving away from home for a first job in a large city, with some 'day release' at technical college to allow you to continue your training).

What types of accommodation are available?

1a You may have friends or relations who will be able to offer you a spare room in their house or flat. In this case you will probably be charged a rent; this could include your breakfast and evening meal.

1b There may be facilities available through the college to find accommodation with a 'landlady' who has registered with the college. You will be charged rent, which may include some meals.

2 Furnished or unfurnished rooms might be available in a house for which the landlord must provide a rent book to record payment. This type of accommodation is often called a 'bed-sit'.

3 You may choose to rent a house or flat with a group of other young people as a joint venture. In this case all the expenses will be shared.

4 Local authorities provide accommodation to rent in the form of houses and flats. To qualify for this you must get your name onto a waiting list. This can be done when you are seventeen years old, but you will not qualify until you are eighteen. The awarding of council accommodation is usually done on a points system which takes into account your personal circumstances, length of time you have lived in the area, and so on. If you are able to get such accommodation allocated to you, the rent will probably be less than that of a private landlord.

Figure 6.3
A place of your own.

Q 8

Study your local newspapers and make a survey of the types of accommodation which are available in the area. Discuss as a group, and then list, the advantages, disadvantages, and possibilities of:

a lodging with a friend or landlady
b renting a furnished 'bed-sit' alone
c renting a furnished flat/house with friends
d renting a council flat.

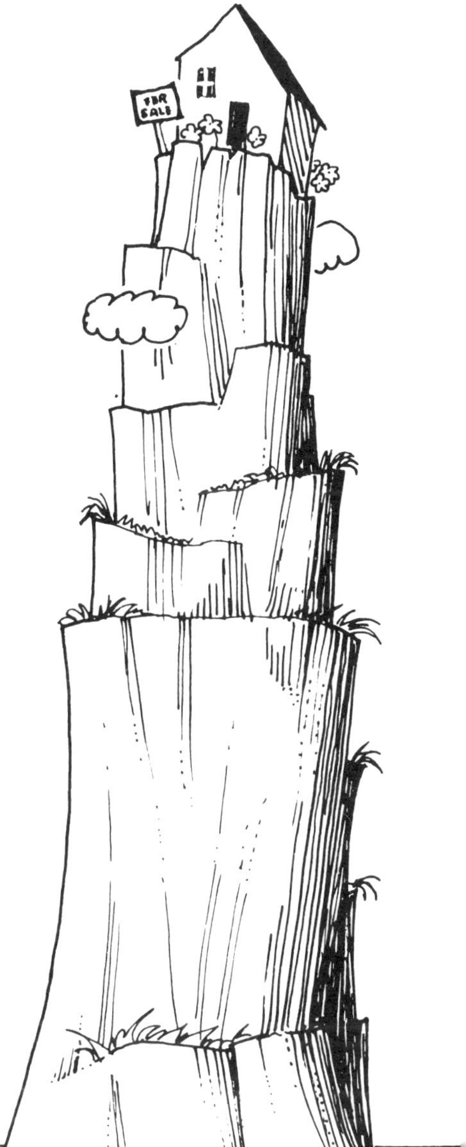

6.5 BUYING A HOUSE OR FLAT

At some point you might be able to consider buying a house or flat. The purchase of a home of your own may be the biggest financial undertaking of your life. In order to consider such an investment you need sufficient money for a deposit and must be confident that you will be able to maintain the repayments on any form of loan which you take out. Because the bank or building society which lends money for house purchase needs to be sure that they will get their money back, they make certain that borrowers do earn enough money to be able to repay the loan over the agreed period of time. If you are able to consider buying a house or flat of your own, then you will have to consider the following factors:

Finance

1 Whether you have enough money for the deposit.
2 Additional purchase costs, including valuation fee, stamp duty, surveyor's fee, solicitor's fee.
3 Whether you can afford to pay back a loan regularly from your wage or salary.
4 The expenses of food, clothing, and shelter (section 6.3).
5 Whether you can afford to furnish the property.
6 Whether you have enough money to maintain the property in good repair.
7 Whether you can afford the additional costs of rates and insurance (discussed later in this section).

Type of property
1 A small one-bedroomed flat might be sufficient for your immediate needs.
2 Many new housing estates are being built with 'starter homes'.
3 An older-type terraced house might be worth considering, particularly if it qualifies for 'improvement grants'.

Q 9
What is a 'starter home'? Investigate locally and obtain information on such developments.

Q 10
What is an 'improvement grant'? Visit your local council offices and obtain details.

Situation
1 Whether the property is in a district which you find attractive.
2 What local amenities exist for shopping, services, transport, and leisure activites.

Taking out a mortgage
As a first-time buyer of a property, you will probably require a loan to purchase the property. As you will have discovered, this is usually obtained by taking out a mortgage through any of the following agencies:
a building society
the local authority
a bank
an insurance company.

To agree to this mortgage the lender will have to consider:
your age
your income
the type and age of the property which you are hoping to buy.

The loan is based on your gross income at the basic rate, that is, without overtime and bonuses.

If the loan is to be to a couple, it will be based on the higher of the two incomes (in certain situations part of the second income may be taken into consideration). The loan is usually in the region of two to two-and-a-half times the considered income for the year and based on repayment over twenty-five years.

The person taking out the mortgage should ensure that, in the event of their death, arrangements have been made to pay the balance due on the mortgage to the lender. A mortgage protection policy like this protects their family.

Q 11
Find out what information you can about the following types of mortgage
a repayment
b endowment
c low-cost endowment
d option.
Find out what tax relief is available on mortgage interest payments.

To purchase a house or flat you will need to establish a plan of action. There are a number of people whom you will need to contact:
an estate agent
a surveyor
a solicitor.

Q 12
Describe briefly what part each of the three people above play in the purchase of a property.

As you found out earlier, there are additional costs to be considered in running your own home.

Rates
This is a tax which is paid to the local council. The local council is also supported by additional grants from the Government. The rates pay for a number of services which we often take for granted.

Q 13
What services does your local council provide from the rate-payers' money?

The sum demanded in the rates is based upon the value of the property — its 'rateable value'. It is based on the size of and amenities provided by the dwelling, and an assessment of the rent that could be charged if the property were let.

Water rates
The water rate is levied by the local water authority (except in Scotland, where it is included in the general rates). The domestic water rate is based on the rateable value of the property. It can be paid in a variety of ways, one of which is payment for the actual amount of water you use. This would be calculated on readings from the water meter installed by the local water authority.

Q 14
Work out the actual rates, including water rates, payable on some of the properties for which you have collected details.

Insurance
If you have taken out a loan or mortgage to purchase a property, you will be required by the lender to pay an insurance premium regularly to insure the 'fabric' of the building. In addition to this, you might be advised to take out a house contents insurance policy. This will provide a sum of money for replacement in the event of loss, theft, fire, or water damage. House contents insurance policies can be written to take account of the individual situation.

Services
Services are discussed in greater detail in later chapters. They include drains and sewage, water supply, fuels (gas, electricity, solid fuel, oil), telephone and postal services, and deliveries of milk and newspapers.

6.6
ALTERNATIVES

At the beginning of this chapter a range of types of accommodation was discussed. You might now like to consider some alternative forms of 'shelter'.

Q 15

a Look around the area in which you live and see if you can find some alternative or unusual types of accommodation.
b As a group, discuss and list the advantages and disadvantages of each type of accommodation which you have found.

Q 16

Discuss why you might choose to live in one of the alternative types of accommodation which you have found out about.

6.7
THE STATE AND HOUSING

The Government services are each administered by separate departments. The Department of the Environment is responsible for housing. The Treasury looks after taxation policy.

Q 17

There are six main Government departments. Find out their names and list the services for which each of these is responsible.

Legislation

A great deal of legislation has been passed to ensure that housing protects its occupants and provides adequate shelter for them.

Q 18

Find out about the Housing Repairs and Rent Act (1974). List briefly what it stated to be the minimum basic standards.

Improvement grants

These were mentioned in section 6.5. These are grants which are available from local authorities under certain conditions. They include money for such things as: inside lavatory, wash-basin, bath/shower, hot and cold water, and repairs and replacements such as roof, woodwork, rewiring, and conversions for disabled people.

Q 19

a Collect information from an estate agent on a small two-bedroomed property which would qualify for an improvement grant in your locality.
b Talk to local people in the trade and try to estimate the likely cost of completing the renovations and improvements.
c Work out the capital sum you would need in order to purchase and make the house ready for occupation.

Figure 6.5
'Alternative accommodation.'

6.8
RENTING A HOME

At the beginning of this chapter you discussed a variety of ways of providing shelter for yourself. Renting accommodation was one solution. Such accommodation is available through private landlords, voluntary concerns, and the local authority.

Private landlords
These may either be individuals or companies which specialize in providing accommodation. Such accommodation is let either furnished or unfurnished, and the rent may be regulated or controlled.

Q 20
From information available in your area, find out about the rent charged for the following types of accommodation in the private sector:
a tied houses
b small terraced or town cottage properties
c conversion of large houses into flats or bed-sits
d purpose-built flats or bed-sits.

Voluntary concerns
There are two ways in which voluntary concerns might provide accommodation:
Charitable trusts are usually formed by organizations connected with a church, philanthropic individuals or groups, bequests, or a big company providing accommodation for its employees.
Housing associations are groups of people who come together and take advantage of Government subsidies which help to maintain a 'fair' rent. Housing corporations have been established by the Government to supervise the work of registered organizations.

Local authority housing
As you found out earlier, the local authority has the responsibility for providing accommodation for those people who have nowhere to live.

Q 21
Survey the types of local authority provision in your area. If possible, find out the typical rent of such accommodation.

Q 22
What did the Housing Act (1980) do to protect tenants of rented property?

Rents
There is now a great deal of legislation to ensure that any rent charged is a fair one.

Q 23
Find out about the following:
a controlled rents
b regulated rents
c rent assessment committees
d rent tribunals
e rent books.

Lease
A lease is a signed agreement between landlord and tenant.

Q 24
Find out what a lease should contain.

Financial assistance from the local authority
The Government has provided the facility for local authorities to assist persons to obtain and maintain adequate shelter for themselves and their families.

Rent rebates are available for tenants of the local authority.
Rent allowances are available for tenants in the private sector. Such rebates and allowances vary with each local authority and are calculated in terms of gross income, rent payable, and a 'needs allowance' which is based on individual circumstances.
Rate rebates are available for people who are purchasing or who own their property. The circumstances under which such rebates are allocated vary in each local authority; for example, to an elderly person with diminished income, or to single-parent families.

Q 25
Find out what financial assistance is available from your local authority.

BACKGROUND READING

IT ISN'T THAT EASY . . .
It isn't always easy finding somewhere to live. Most of the cities of the World have their share of young people who have come looking for work and independence from their families and instead have found little but a cold pavement.

In Britain, the problem has been getting worse in recent years. Organizations like the Cyrenians and the Salvation Army provide shelter for thousands of homeless people every night. Their normal clients are the 'down and outs'; these are men (and they are nearly all men not women) who are unable or unwilling to cope with living in a house or flat. Now the shelter organizations find that they have increasingly to deal with young people whose principal problems are their inexperience of life and their inability to find work.

Thousands of young people arrive in London every year. Many of them end up in very unsatisfactory bed and breakfast accommodation, sharing a room with several others and forced to be out all day long, summer or winter. And this may cost about three-quarters of the wage the young people earn, if they have a job.

There are some organizations set up specifically to try to help people in this predicament. One of these is the Nucleus Housing Association in Earl's Court. This area is attractive to young people, but it has the highest population density in London and a very serious housing problem. Nucleus provide the few people they are able to help with a place to live for a few months at a reasonable price while they find work, learn to fend for themselves, and make friends in the area. They do this by borrowing houses that are awaiting renovation or conversion into flats and which might otherwise stand empty for up to two years.

This work is expensive. Nucleus have to pay rent to the owners, rates, electricity bills, and so on. They are mainly dependent for their income on the 'rent' which their 'tenants' pay to them. There are other difficulties too. Usually the people they house have not been away from home before and they may find independence much harder work than they had imagined. They have to learn how to manage their money so as to be able to pay for their food and accommodation, how to get on with others when space is limited, and how to keep their rooms reasonably clean.

Nucleus stress that they can only help a tiny proportion of those who come to them. Their message to anyone who might be thinking of leaving home and arriving in a city with nowhere to go is — don't!

Figure 6.6

CHAPTER 7
The home as a building

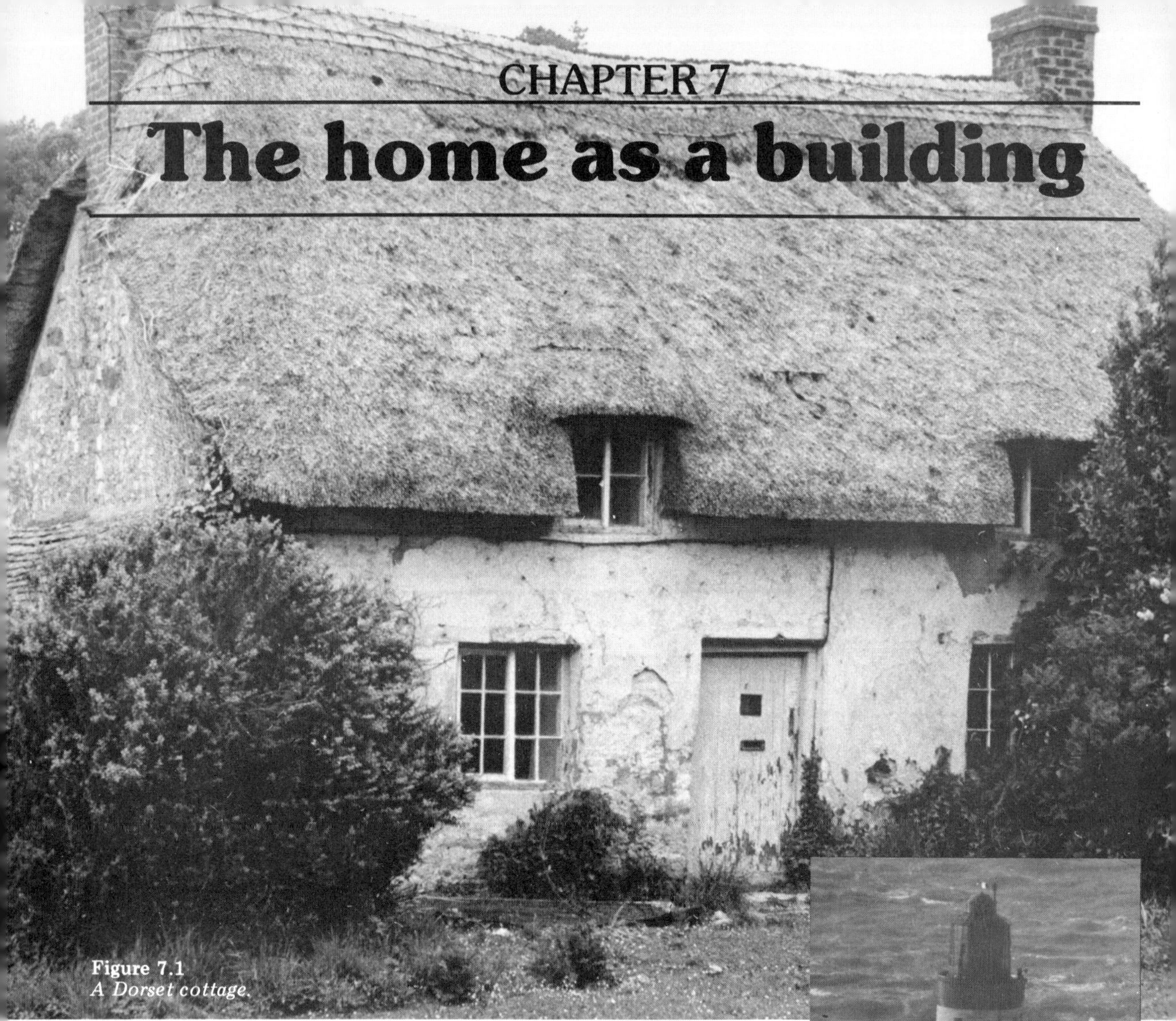

Figure 7.1
A Dorset cottage.

Figure 7.2
The Needles Lighthouse, off the western tip of the Isle of Wight. (The light is 24 m above the high (spring) tide mark, and can be seen 27 km away; the lighthouse has three men on duty with a rota of 28 days on, and 28 days off.)

7.1
THE SHELL

Our remote ancestors lived in rough huts or occasionally in caves. These were their 'shells' which protected them from enemies and the elements. Nowadays we expect more comfort and build purpose-built 'shells'. Today's buildings and other structures come in many shapes and sizes, and have many uses.

Q 1

Look at figure 7.1, 7.2, and 7.3 and at figures 1.2 to 1.7 on pages 4 and 5.

a Which of these do you think show 'homes'?
b Which of these would you call 'buildings'?
c Which are intended to be permanent?

In Britain the law requires a home to be a building which is made to last and is fit for human habitation. Different standards of construction are set for buildings which are lived in and for those which have other purposes.

In the past, houses were built of local materials. Some regions had good building stone; others clay suitable for bricks. Where there was neither, materials such as 'cob' (a rough plaster made with clay, gravel, and straw) or timber were used.

As you learned in Chapter 1, a structure of bricks, wood, and tiles is not a home, but a place where a home can begin. And although a house may be designed by an architect and built by a professional builder, it still has to be maintained. Whether you live in a house or flat, you need to understand how it is constructed so as to be able to identify any faults that might occur.

Look at the diagram in figure 7.4. You will see that the foundations of a modern house are usually made of concrete, at least one metre deep and twice as thick as the walls. The outer walls of the house are built of two layers separated by an air cavity. A damp-proof course, usually made of bitumen strip, is inserted just above ground level. Bricks behave like blotting paper, and its purpose is to stop the damp rising from the ground up the walls and into the fabric of the house.

The internal walls may be built of one layer of bricks or cement blocks, but more often they are 'stud walls', constructed of a timber frame covered with plasterboard (studding). Those made of brick or blocks may or may not support the floor and the roof. If they do, they are said to be load-bearing. (Timber-framed internal walls are never load-bearing.) When holes are made in brick walls for doors or windows, the gap is bridged by a cement or metal lintel which supports the bricks above.

Q 2

Figure 7.5 shows a cavity wall. Explain the function of the butterfly-shaped pieces of wire. Fibreglass mats are sometimes inserted into the cavity: what do you think they are for?

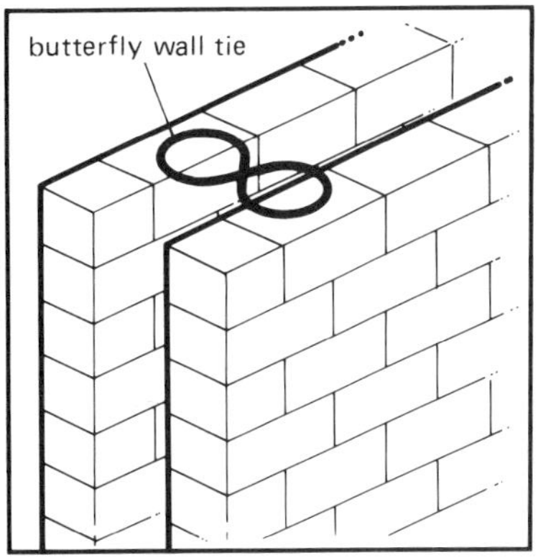

Figure 7.5a
Cavity wall with butterfly ties.

Figure 7.5b
Cavity wall in course of construction, with fibreglass mat in position.

Figure 7.3
Permanent holiday caravans.

Figure 7.4
The foundations and outer walls of a modern house, with a suspended timber ground floor.

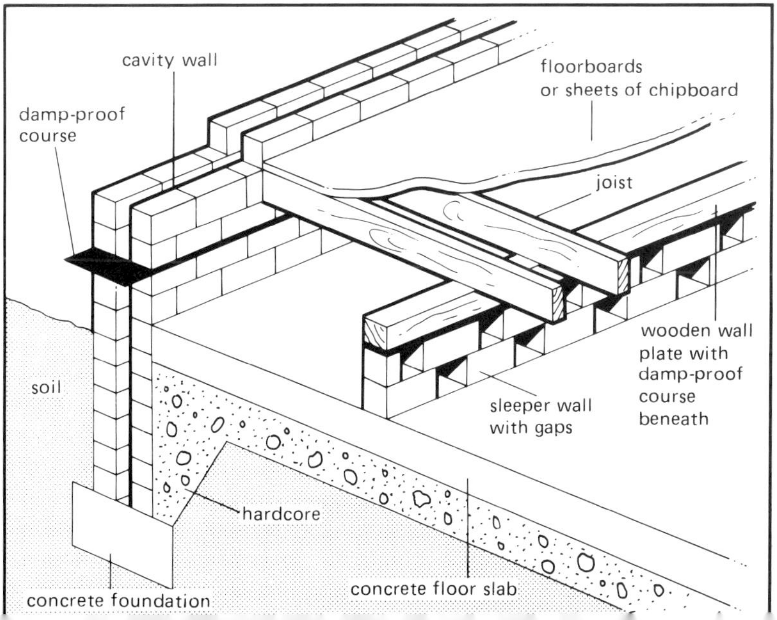

Q 3
How do you think you could tell which walls are load-bearing and which are non-load-bearing in a house for which you do not have the plans?

In modern houses the ground floor is either solid concrete which may then be covered with tiles, or it is made of wood planks (floor-boards) at right-angles to wooden joists. Floors of upstairs rooms are suspended; they consist of planks or large sheets of chipboard suspended on the joists. Plasterboard attached to the underside makes the ceiling of the room beneath.

The typical roof comes to a point and is called a pitched roof. It is constructed of timber struts carefully designed so that the minimum of wood gives maximum support. The roof rafters are covered with bituminous felt and then tiles are laid on top. To prevent water dripping down the house walls, the tiles at the edge of the roof project over the gutters. Where holes are made in the roof for windows, pipes, or chimneys, L-shaped pieces of metal (flashing) need to be fixed around them to make the roof watertight. (See figure 7.8.)

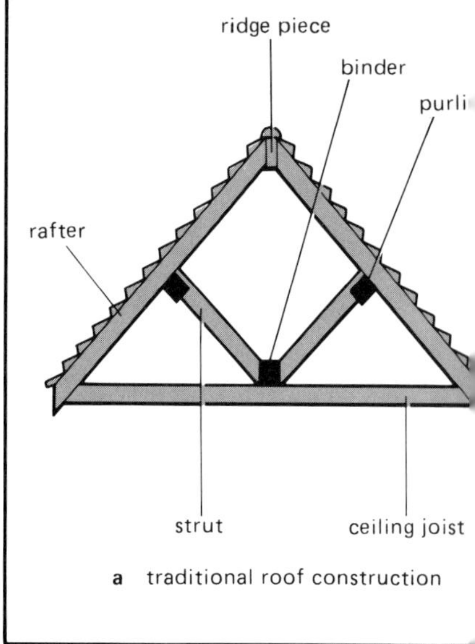

Figure 7.6
Roof construction.

7.2
PLANNING SPACE

Most people expect a house or flat to have at least one bedroom, a bathroom, a living-room, and a kitchen. In many houses, the kitchen and bathroom are one above the other. The staircase usually occupies one side of the house, with the bedrooms and living rooms taking up the other side. Within these basic limitations, space can still be arranged in various ways for various purposes.

Q 4
One variation is the choice between a bathroom combined with, or separate from, the lavatory. List all the advantages and disadvantages that you can think of for these two arrangements.

Q 5
What restrictions might govern the relative positions of a downstairs kitchen and an upstairs bathroom?

Few of us have the chance of planning our ideal house. Sometimes it might be possible to modify an existing house or flat by removing or putting up extra walls, and so change the size of rooms to suit individual needs. It may also be possible to add on extra rooms, garages, or conservatories. What may appeal to the young and childless may not suit the needs of a family or older people, and this is an important point to consider when choosing a house to buy.

1 Find out what planning permission is necessary and how it can be obtained in your area.

2 Make a list of those things which require permission and those which do not.

Figure 7.8
Flashing prevents leakage around the chimney.

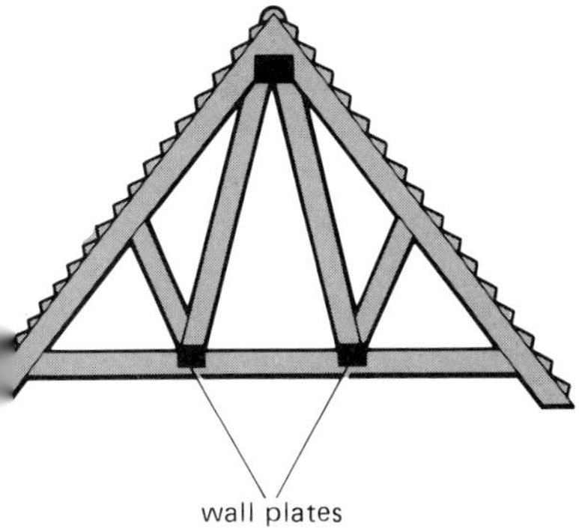

b modern lightweight trussed roof section (factory built)

Figure 7.7
Constructing the roof.

Your teacher will show you a copy of the plans of a typical pair of semi-detached houses (worksheet PM9). The arrangement of the rooms is fairly standard, but minor variations are possible.

Q 6
The living-room of one house is longer than that of the adjoining house. How has this been achieved? (Note that the bedroom above is the same size as the one next door.)

When the family who live in this house first moved in, they consisted of two parents and two young children. They bought the house before it was built, so they had some say in the planning of the internal space.

Q 7
The family asked for a wide entrance hall instead of a narrow passage. Write down as many reasons as you can think of for their request.

Q 8
Originally, the builder intended to make one through room instead of the two separate living-rooms shown on the plans. List the reasons why the family asked for separate living and dining-rooms.

As the children grew older, the accommodation became inadequate; they needed a quiet place in which to study and entertain friends away from the family living space. This was achieved by having an extension to the first floor built over the garage of the same width and length as the garage and extending from the front to the back of the house.

Q 9
What would you have put into this extension and how would you have organized the space? Draw a plan of the extension as a guide for an architect.

Q 10
The living-rooms of the adjoining houses are adjacent and so there might be a problem from noise. What could be done about this, and what might be the drawbacks to the alternative arrangements?

Q 11
How could you get natural light to the upstairs landing?

Note the aspect of the house. The kitchen and living-room face south-west and the dining-room faces north-east.

Q 12
How will this affect living and working conditions in the house?

Q 13
List all the advantages you can think of in having a kitchen which overlooks the back garden.

Some houses do have the kitchen at the front of the house, and the living-room and dining-room at the back. All you have to do is to turn the original plan through 180°.

Figure 7.9
If water escapes it can do a lot of damage ... make sure you know how to turn off the supply quickly.

Figure 7.10a
The older direct plumbing system.

Q 14
How will this affect the aspect and quality of the rooms?

These are some of the many factors that enter into the choice of living arrangement; compromises always have to be made.

7.3 WATER AND DRAINS

Water is an essential service, but it has to be controlled in pipes. If it escapes, it can do a lot of damage. It is therefore vital to understand how the system works so that faults can be detected, the supply can be switched off in an emergency, and the best equipment can be selected.

The plumbing system consists of two parts: the water supply and the waste system.

WATER SUPPLY

At the point where the service pipe to the house leaves the water authority's main, there is an underground tap (stopcock) covered by a small metal plate. This is usually found immediately outside the boundary of the property. Beyond that point the pipework belongs to, and is the responsibility of, the householder. It enters the house vertically as the rising main and often has a second stopcock beneath the kitchen sink. From this point it travels to the cold-water cistern in the loft, after giving off a branch pipe to the kitchen sink. The cistern supplies the hot-water cylinder which is usually directly below it.

There are two systems of pipe-work for supplying water to different parts of the house: the modern indirect system and the older direct system (see figures 7.10a and b).

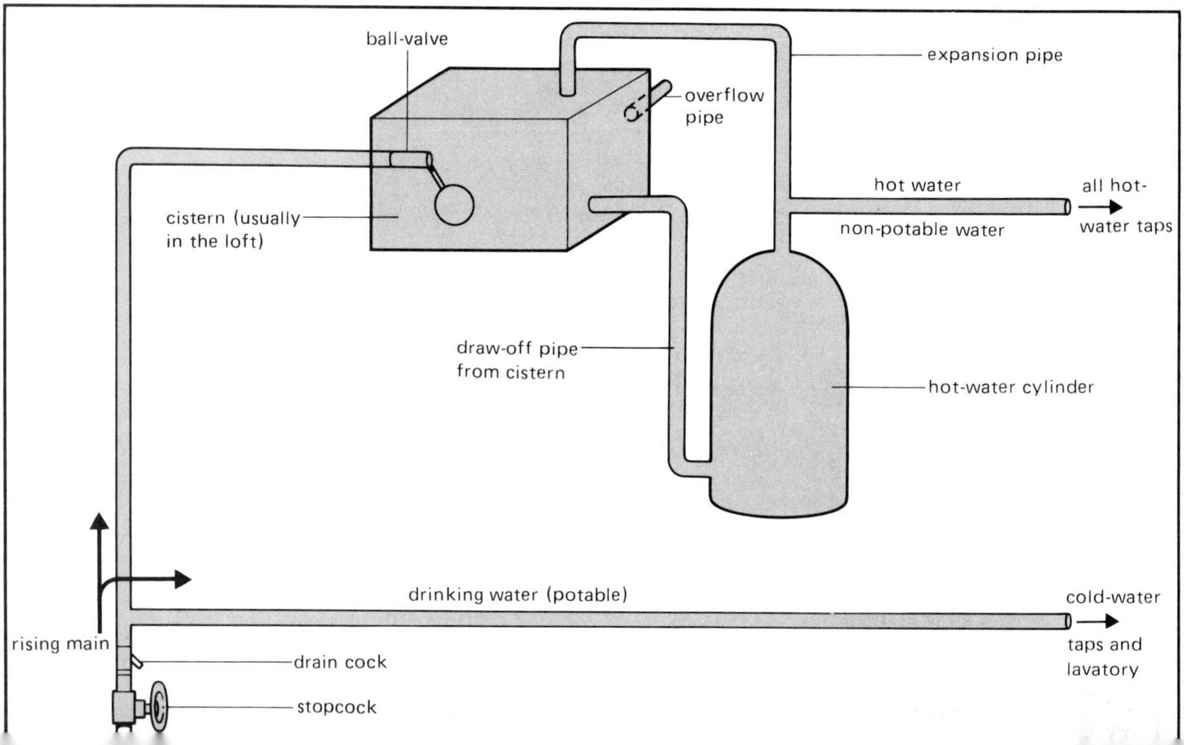

Q 15

There are several reasons why the modern indirect system is superior to the direct system. Look at figure 7.10 carefully and list the reasons.

At various points in the plumbing system, automatic valves are used to control the water supply. If they fail, overflow pipes channel the water through the house to the outside.

Hand-operated taps are, of course, needed for kitchen sinks, wash-basins, and baths. The commonest type is the rising spindle tap which allows water to flow as the spindle raises the washer (see figure 7.11). Stop-valves are yet another type of tap, but their function is to prevent or allow the flow of water along a pipe. They work in a similar way to ordinary taps and have washers (see figure 7.12).

1 Locate all the stopcocks in your own home.

2 Try to find out what they do (but do not turn them on and off!)

3 Make a labelled diagram of the water system.

In an emergency, it is sometimes possible to shut off isolated sections rather than the entire system. Houses of different ages and complexity of plumbing vary greatly as to the number of stopcocks provided: modern houses usually have more than older ones.

Q 16

Imagine that the cold-water tap in the kitchen sink has stuck in the open position, so that water pours out and it cannot be turned off. What action would you take to stop the flow?

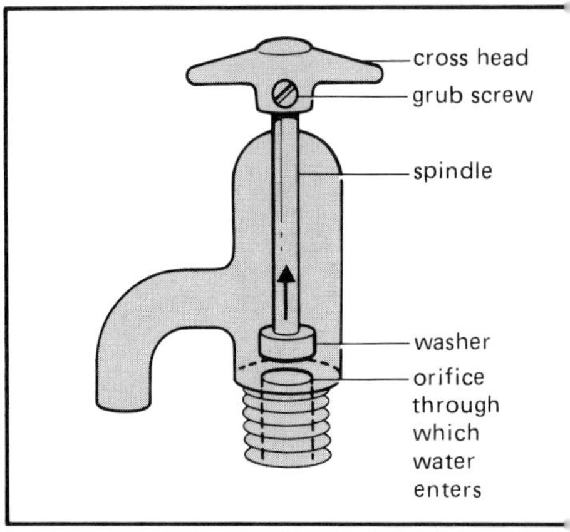

Figure 7.11
A standard rising spindle tap.

Figure 7.12
A stop-valve.

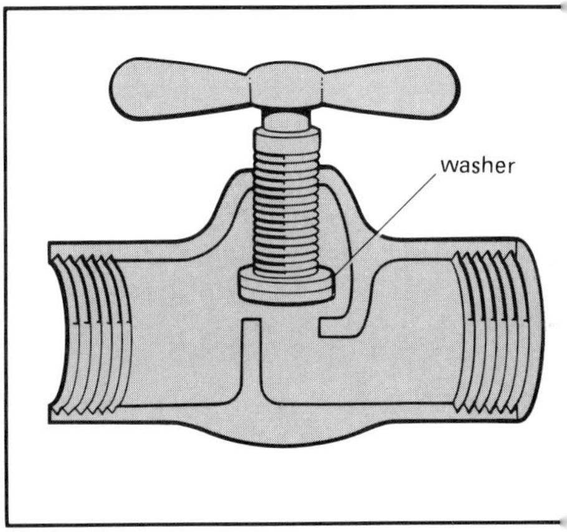

Figure 7.10b
Modern indirect plumbing system.

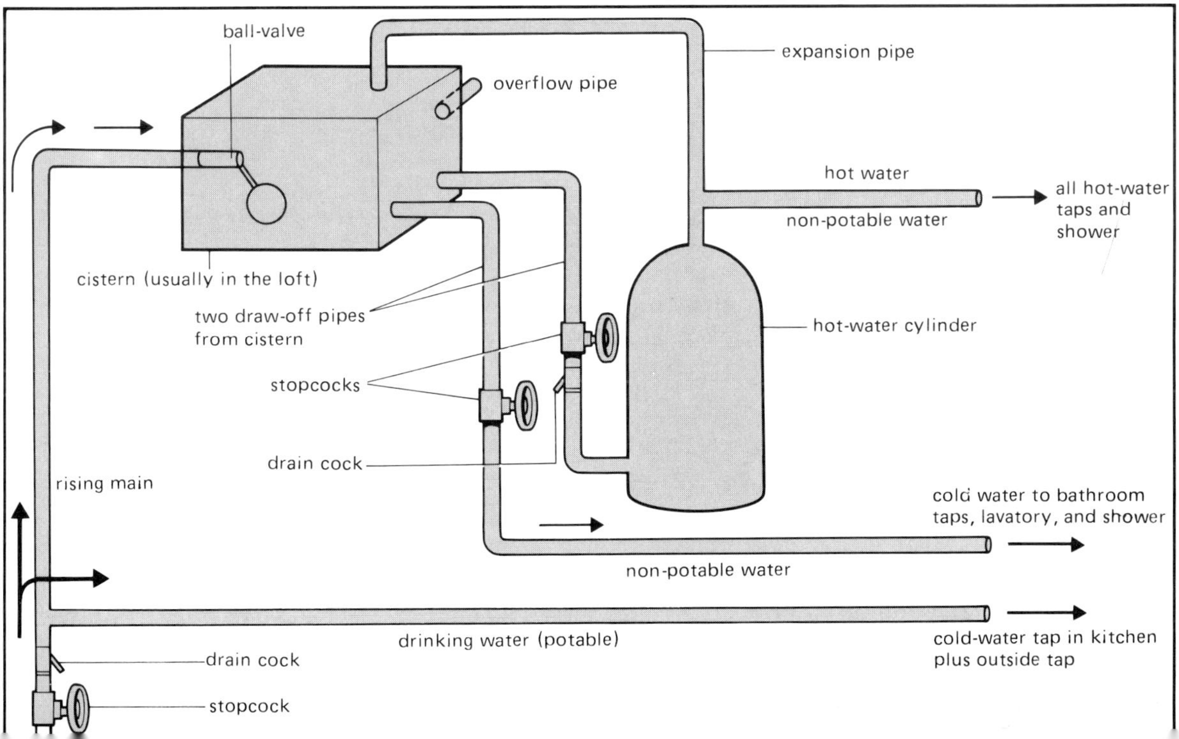

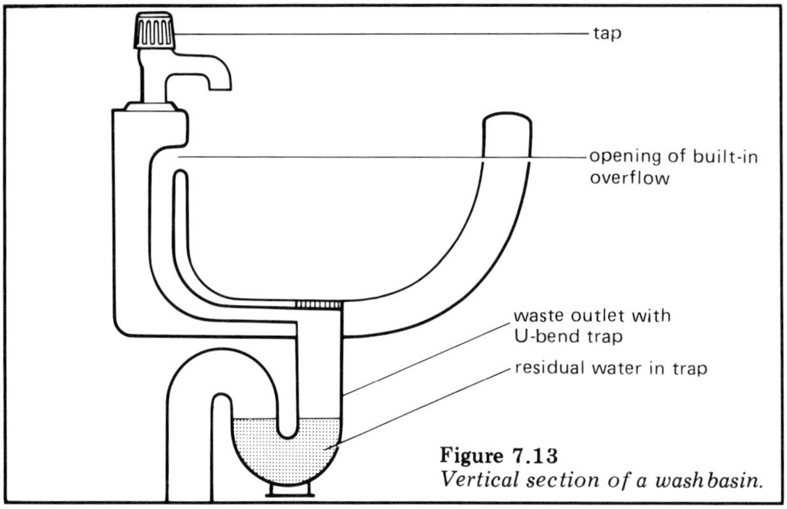

Figure 7.13
Vertical section of a washbasin.

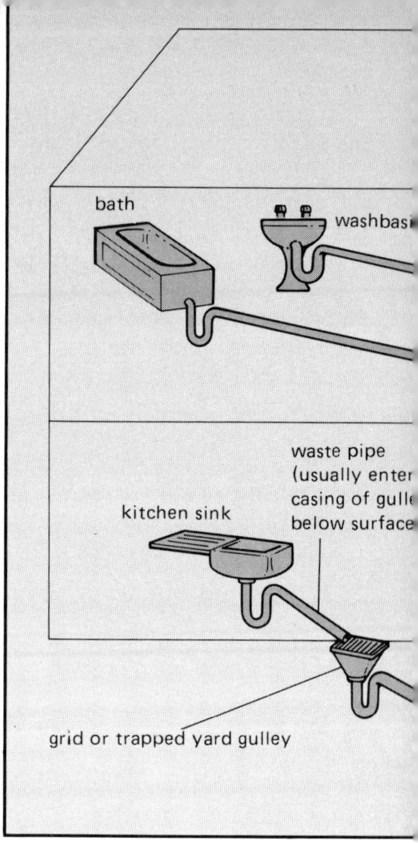

Figure 7.14a
Modern single-stack waste system, hidden from view by being built into the house.

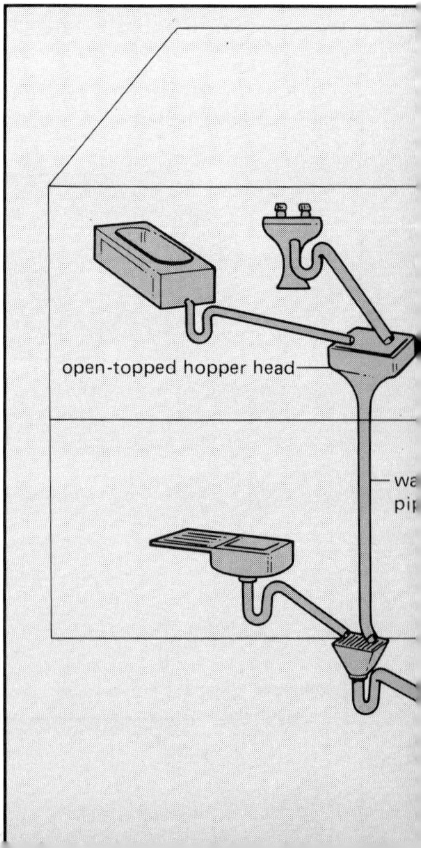

Q 17
Imagine that water is pouring through an upstairs bedroom ceiling owing to a fault connected with the cold-water cistern in the loft. Explain the possible causes of the flooding. What action would you take to stop it?

Q 18
A washer in a hot-water tap needs repair. How would you cut off the water supply to the tap, if there is no stopcock in the draw-off pipe leading from the cold-water cistern to the hot-water cylinder?

Central heating systems may be connected to the water supply. You will learn about them in Chapter 8.

THE WASTE SYSTEM

So far we have only considered the supply of water: at the other end is the disposal of wastes. Wastes are piped to the underground sewer in the road, the connecting pipes running from the house to the sewer in straight lines. Whenever there is a change of direction, an inspection chamber or 'rodding point' is provided. This allows cleaning rods to be inserted in case of blockage. Rain water from gutters does not empty into the sewer as it could overload it. Instead it is piped to a 'soakaway'. As the digging of drains is quite expensive, architects put kitchens and bathrooms close together so that one drain serves both.

Houses in rural areas may not be on the main drainage system. In this case there are two alternatives for waste disposal: 'cesspools' and 'septic tanks'. Septic tanks and cesspools allow for the breakdown of solid matter by the natural action of micro-organisms. Cesspools are open to the air and therefore said to be *aerobic*. Septic tanks are sealed units, that is, little air penetrates them and the breakdown is called *anaerobic*. The resulting effluent can safely be allowed to drain away.

Q 19
Why should a household with a septic tank be careful not to use excessive amounts of disinfectants or detergents?

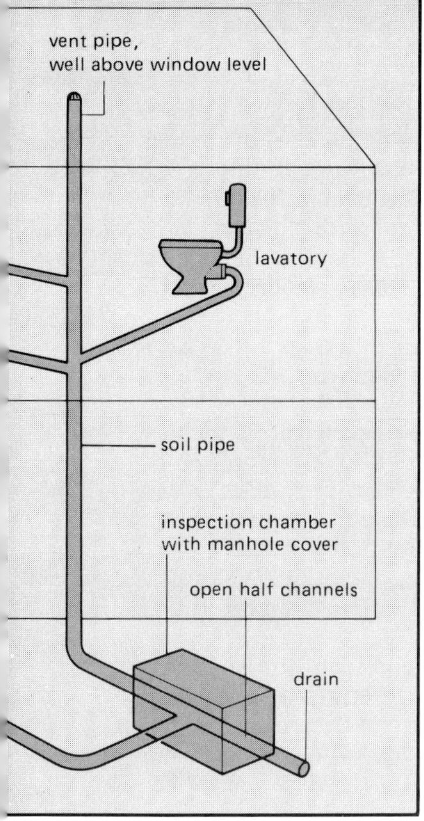

Figure 7.14b
Older two-pipe waste system, usually visible on outside of house.

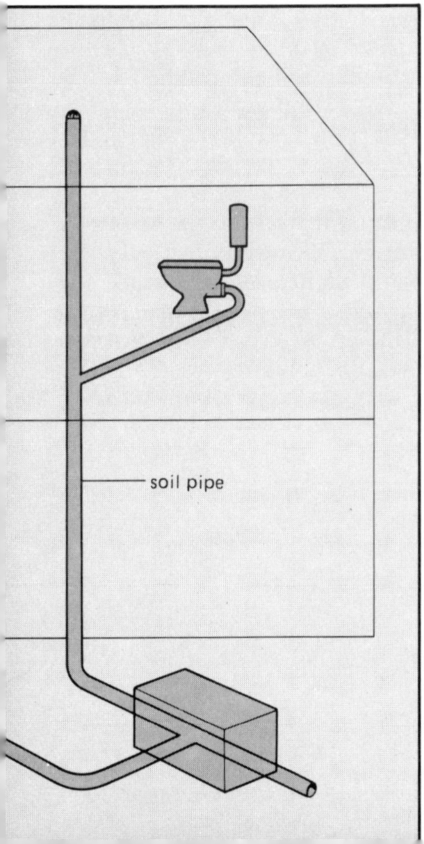

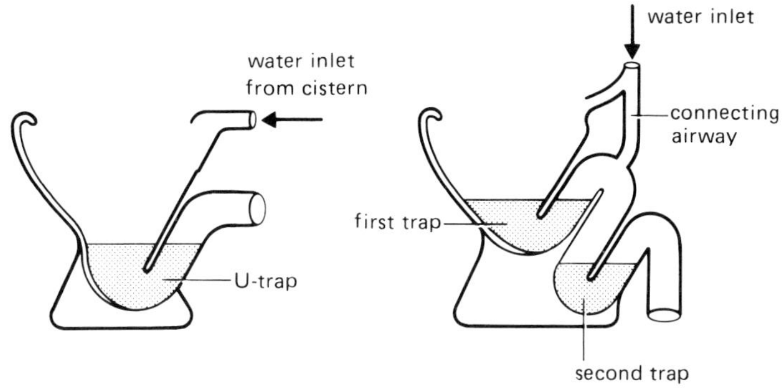

Figure 7.15
Two different types of lavatory.

In order to stop drain smells from entering the house, all waste outlets from lavatories, washbasins, and baths are provided with water-filled traps which act as an air seal. Figure 7.13 shows the U-bend trap of a washbasin. Notice the screw plug which is provided for cleaning, and the built-in overflow.

All trapped waste outlets empty into vertical pipes which are connected to the underground drain. Most houses built since about 1960 have a single-stack (single-pipe) waste system which is usually built into the structure and thus hidden from view. You will see that most outlets empty into a vertical open-topped soil pipe, but the kitchen waste empties into a grid or trapped yard gulley. (See figure 7.14.)

Q 20
Why is the soil pipe always open at the top?

Washing-machines and dish-washers, unlike basins and baths, are movable, but they still discharge waste water. The simplest answer is to hook the curved waste pipe over the edge of the kitchen sink, but this hinders the sink's use for other purposes. It is much more convenient to have both waste and water supply permanently plumbed in.

Perhaps the most important appliance of the waste disposal system is the lavatory. It needs to deliver a strong flush with automatic filling of the cistern. A ball valve similar to that of the cold-water cistern takes care of the latter. There are two different mechanisms for providing the flush. The first is the old-fashioned high-level bell flush wash-down with a chain. The second is the modern double-trap siphonic type. The two types are shown in figure 7.15.

Q 21
a Why is the double-trap siphonic pan more efficient than the wash-down type?
b How does it work?

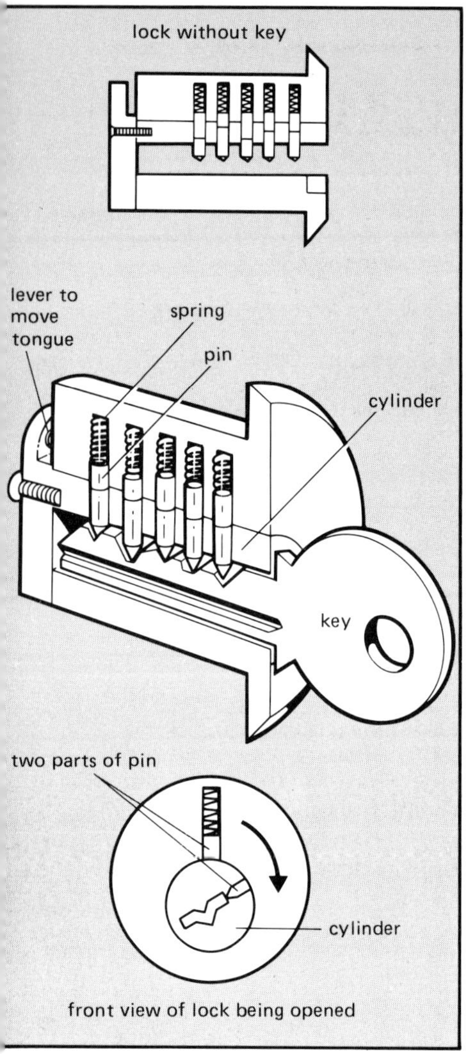

Figure 7.16
A Yale-type pin-tumbler lock. The cylinder is stopped from moving by pins pushed down by springs. Each pin is cut into two parts, all in different places. When the key is pushed in, it raises the pins so that the cuts line up with the edge of the cylinder; it can then turn and move a lever to pull back the lock tongue (which is not shown here).

BACKGROUND READING

HOW TO GIVE BURGLARS A HARD TIME

Most burglars are not skilled professionals working at night. They wait till you go out of the house, and then quickly try the doors and windows. Often one of these has been left unlocked and they can just walk in, pick up your video recorder and leave. But if they can't get in straight away, they are likely to give up. So quite simple measures will prevent most burglaries.

The first is just to be careful to lock all doors and windows when you go out: easy, but easily forgotten.

However, some locks are simple to open without the key. You really can open a plain Yale-type lock with a credit card, by pushing it between door and frame to force back the tongue. Every outside door should have a deadlock, which can't be forced and can only be locked and unlocked with a key. Of course the back door must have as good a lock as the front; and you have to remember to lock both whenever you go out.

Simple window catches can be forced from the outside in seconds. For example, all that is needed for a sash window catch is a knife blade inserted between the sashes. So proper window locks should be fitted, and always done up when the window is shut.

More drastic measures include all kinds of electronic alarms. However, if a burglar really wants to get in you probably can't stop him. So it is sensible to take other precautions. Valuables should not be put where they can be easily seen through front windows, and anything really expensive like jewellery should not be kept in obvious places like dressing-table drawers. Cash should not be kept at home. And you can ask the police to mark your goods with an invisible ink that glows under ultra-violet light. They will also advise you on locks and other security precautions.

If you go away on holiday and forget to stop the milk or the newspapers, a burglar is likely to notice them piling up. He knows he has the run of the house and plenty of time to take everything of value. When you go away, it is a good idea to tell neighbours and the police, who will keep an eye on the place. Some towns have 'neighbourhood watch' schemes, where all residents keep an eye for anything suspicious and report it to the police.

CHAPTER 8

Thinking about energy

8.1
OUR NEED FOR FUELS

One of the functions of our homes is to protect us from the outside world, to provide a kind of 'personal habitat'. We like to be able to control the temperature and lighting, and so energy is needed to warm us in winter and sometimes to cool us in summer. When sunlight is not available we use energy to provide lighting. We use energy to cool food down (in refrigerators and freezers) and to heat it up (cooking). In addition, a little energy is needed to run labour-saving equipment.

Figure 8.1
Most energy in the home is used for heating.

Q 1

a Make a list of all the uses of energy in the home that you can think of.
b For each one, write down where the energy comes from (electricity, gas, oil, coal, and so on).

This energy is usually readily available. You may not have considered from where and how this energy comes, but you should be aware of what it costs.

Figure 8.2
a *Wind power has been used for centuries, but the amount of energy provided is small.*
b *Energy from moving water: the Rance tidal power station on the coast of France.*

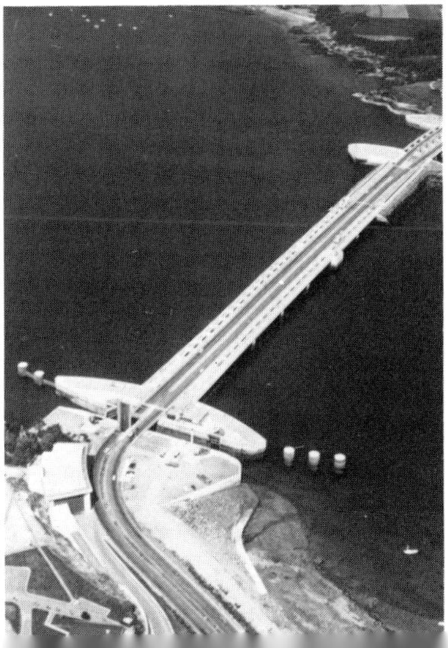

8.2
WHERE DOES ENERGY COME FROM?

Energy comes mainly from fossil fuels (gas, coal, and oil). They were formed millions of years ago and are now being used up, that is, they are non-renewable sources of energy. We also have nuclear energy made in a nuclear power station, and energy (in small amounts) from such natural phenomena as the Sun, wind, waterfalls, and tides. Hydro-electric power (HEP) stations are used in areas where the power of moving water can be controlled and used.

All the fuels and other sources of energy can be used to provide electricity. This is normally done in fuel-burning power stations, in nuclear power stations, or in hydro-electric plants. Electricity is the same no matter where the energy that provides it comes from.

Although gas and electricity are often classified together, and their uses are compared later in this chapter, they are actually quite different things. Gas is a fuel which releases energy when it is burned. Electricity is not a fuel and does not burn, although it can make things very hot. It is sometimes called a 'form of energy'.

Q 2

a Where did the energy in gas, coal, and oil come from?
b Why can't we rely on new supplies of these fuels being formed?

8.3
THE ENERGY CRISIS

For most of the history of mankind our energy usage was small. Most work was done using animal and human muscle power. Wood was the principal fuel used. In many parts of the World this is still so. It was only in the nineteenth century that fossil fuels began to be used on a very large scale. (See figure 8.3.) World demand for energy from fuels is still increasing, both because the population is growing and because the proportion of it which uses large amounts of energy is growing.

Q 3
Why is there no mention of electricity in figure 8.3?

Q 4
Look at the use of fuels in 1980 in figure 8.3. How does this relate to the use of fuels in your own class group?

Before 1973, people behaved as though there was an endless supply of cheap fuel. The realization that oil and other fossil fuels are finite (limited as a resource) came in 1973 when OPEC (The Organization of Petroleum Exporting Countries) made the first of many large increases in the price of crude oil. This had a serious effect on the World economy and affected the pockets of everyone.

It is not possible to predict how much fossil fuel remains in terms of years, since too many variable factors are involved. Who can tell what further exploration will discover? Improved technology will certainly help to drain the last recoverable oil from wells, and uneconomic coal mines may yield their last by coal gasification. Oil and natural gas are likely to be the first fossil fuels to be exhausted. Coal resources, however, are vast and can be converted to motor fuel and synthetic natural gas. This and other possibilities may sustain us until fuel-breeding nuclear processes or less environmentally hazardous fusion methods are perfected.

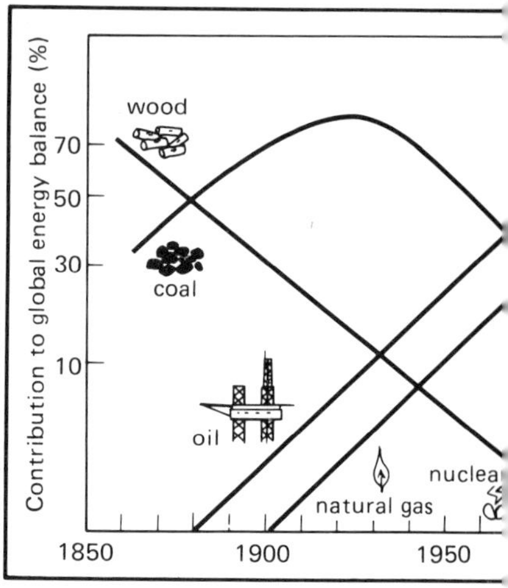

Figure 8.3
The changing importance of primary sources of energy.

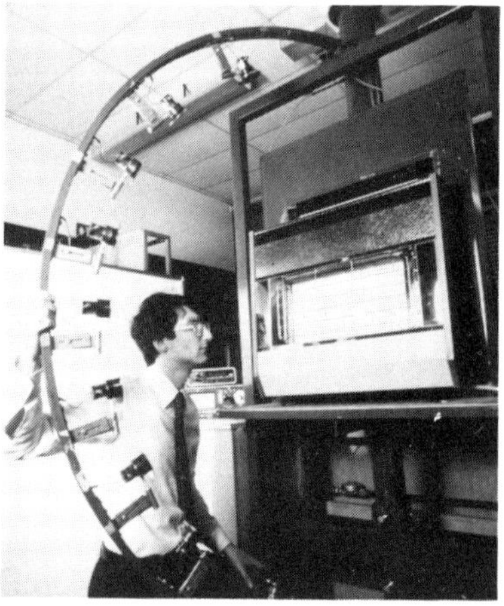

Figure 8.6
Some of the work involved in bringing gas to your home:
a *laying a gas pipe*

8.4
POLLUTION PROBLEMS

As you know, when fuels burn and energy is transferred, the fuel does not just disappear. It is converted by chemical reactions into other things. Some substances formed by combustion, such as carbon dioxide, are harmless as long as they are released into the atmosphere. Here is the equation for natural gas.

CH_4	$+ 2O_2 \longrightarrow$	CO_2	$+ 2H_2O$
natural gas (methane)	oxygen	carbon dioxide	water

Natural gas is by far the cleanest fuel. Most fuels contain impurities of some kind. For instance, low grade fuel oil and certain types of coal contain sulphur. There is increasing concern

Figure 8.4
Waste heat from power stations can be used to heat greenhouses.

Figure 8.5
Research at British Gas:
a *measuring the radiant heat output from a gas fire*
b *studying the way gas ignites and burns.*

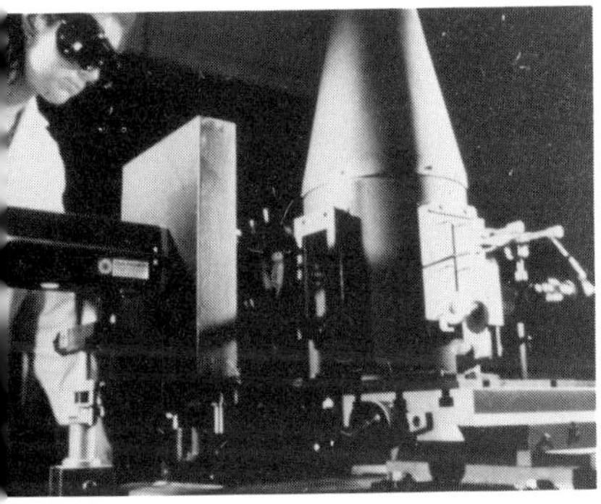

b *finding the position of underground pipes and cables using the Gascopact, an instrument developed by British Gas. It works by detecting the magnetic field induced in metal pipes and cables by the small transmitter placed nearby.*

for the purity of the environment and for the health of people (and other organisms) affected by substances released into the atmosphere.

Q 5
What substances are now giving cause for concern? What are their effects thought to be?

There is another problem too. Fuels must be allowed to burn completely. Boilers and heaters must be properly maintained and have adequate ventilation. This is because oxygen is needed for the chemical reactions involved in burning. (See the equation above.)

Incomplete combustion is dangerous because poisonous chemicals such as carbon monoxide are released into the air as fumes. In addition, efficient flues are needed to prevent your house from filling up with water vapour and pollutants.

8.5
AVAILABLE ENERGY

Most houses in Britain have two sources of energy continuously available: gas and electricity. Virtually 100 per cent of all homes have electricity; 86 per cent have piped gas. Bottled gas, oil, and solid fuel are also available in most areas.

GAS

Gas is transported from below the North Sea across Britain in a network of large pipes at high pressure. In urban areas the pipes are smaller in diameter and the pressure is reduced. Even smaller service pipes take gas from the street mains into the home. Reducing valves make sure that the pressure is correct. To be used efficiently and safely, gas appliances need a steady pressure supplied to them.

Gas is used in the home on a very large scale, as table 8.1 shows.

Q 6
a Make a list of the uses of gas in the home.
b What is gas not used for? Explain why.

Energy source	Percentage used
Gas	57.4
Solid fuel	18.7
Electricity	18.3
Oil	5.6

Table 8.1
Energy use in the home in Britain in 1983.

In Britain, 85 per cent of the energy used in the home is used for space heating and water heating, and much of this is provided by gas.

Figure 8.7
Electricity pylons: on the right is a voltage-reducing substation.

ELECTRICITY

Is the Electricity Board crazy? In a battery-powered device like an electric torch, the flow of electricity is easy to understand. It comes out of one end of the battery, goes through the switch and the bulb, and returns to the other end of the battery to complete the circuit. It is at a low voltage, such as 4.5 V, which is quite safe and could not give you an electric shock. But the torch gives plenty of light.

Voltage is the force which drives electricity around the circuit. You can think of it as like pressure forcing water along a pipe.

Mains electricity comes into most British homes at 240 V. That is enough to kill you — so why not send it in at a safe, low voltage? The starter motor of a car works off the 12 V car battery, yet delivers more power than a washing machine motor.

Mains electricity is in the form of *alternating current*. That means that the flow keeps stopping and then flowing in the opposite direction. In Britain, it reverses 50 times every second. You might think this is quite pointless.

Mains wiring is arranged so that one of the wires is *earthed* — connected to the ground. Although the ground is not made of a material which conducts electricity easily (such as a metal), in fact it is a very good conductor because a flow of electricity through it is not confined as it is in a narrow wire. The thicker a conductor, the less resistance it offers to the flow of electricity. So if you are standing on the ground, and you touch the other, unearthed wire, a lethal 240 V flows through your body to the ground. You may just get a nasty shock. But if you are in good contact with the ground — for example standing on a wet floor — it will kill you. Wetness reduces the electrical resistance of your skin.

So there are three apparently crazy features of mains electricity: high voltage, alternating current, and earthing. You may well wonder why the board doesn't send it to you at a nice, safe 12 V, as direct current (that is, flowing one way, as from a battery) and through two wires neither of which is earthed.

Q 7

Think how thick the wires are which are connected to the 12 V battery of a car. Compare them with the flex of an electrical appliance (remember, this contains three wires, not just one). Can you guess why the mains supply is not at 12 V?

In fact electricity is sent out across the country at an enormous 400 000 V. If it were not at such a high voltage, it would not have the energy to overcome the resistance of all those miles of not very thick wire. Local electricity *substations* have devices called *transformers* which step the voltage down to the level of the ordinary mains supply, so that the electricity has only a couple of miles to travel at this voltage.

A transformer consists basically of two coils of wire, one for the incoming electricity, the other for the outgoing electricity. The two coils are close to each other, but not touching. To understand how the electric current in the first coil produces electricity in the second, take a radio, tune it to a space between stations, and hold it near a light switch. Switch the light on and off a few times. If the radio makes a sound, it shows that a burst of electricity has travelled through space and has made a current flow in the wire coil of the radio's aerial.

Q 8

When does the radio make a sound? Does this explain why mains electricity stops and starts 50 times a second?

Electricity comes into your home along two wires. One is called the *live* wire — this is the one that can give you a shock. The other is the *neutral* wire — this one is connected to earth at the transformer in the substation. Figure 8.8 shows how the wiring of a house is arranged. Look at it before you read on. If the neutral wire were not earthed, you could touch the live wire and not get a shock — unless you were touching the neutral wire as well. You might think you were safe. But in fact, if the wiring inside an appliance comes loose, it is quite possible for the live wire to touch one metal part and make it 'live', and for

Figure 8.8
Simplified diagram of the wiring system of a flat.
The incoming main cable is encased in a metal tube which protects it. The bottom of the tube is sunk deep into the ground so that it makes a good connection with the earth.
The live and neutral wires run to a sealed main service unit *which contains the electricity board's own big fuse, which only board officials can replace, and a double main switch with which they can cut off both the live and the neutral wire to isolate the flat completely if you don't pay your bill. From here the two wires run through the electricity meter to the* consumer unit, *which belongs to the flat owner and contains one main switch and several fuses, one for each of the house circuits. The earth wire runs through an earth connection to the consumer unit.*
Only three house circuits are shown running from the unit; in real life there would be more.

1 The lighting circuit supplies two ceiling lamps hanging from *ceiling roses*, which are circular junction boxes for the wiring. The lamps are controlled by wall switches.

2 The power sockets are supplied by a *ring main*, in which each wire of the circuit runs in a complete loop all round the floor. Thus each socket is connected to the consumer unit by two sets of wiring, which helps to prevent overloading. (Before ring mains were invented, each socket had to have a circuit of its own.)
From one socket, a *spur* (branch) runs off to power a wall heater. This spur has its own fuse and switch set in a box on the wall.

3 An electric cooker uses so much power that it has to have a circuit to itself. The circuit runs to a *cooker unit* on the wall, to which the cooker is connected directly without a plug. The unit also has a power socket, into which you might plug some kitchen appliance. There are two switches, one for the cooker and one for the socket.

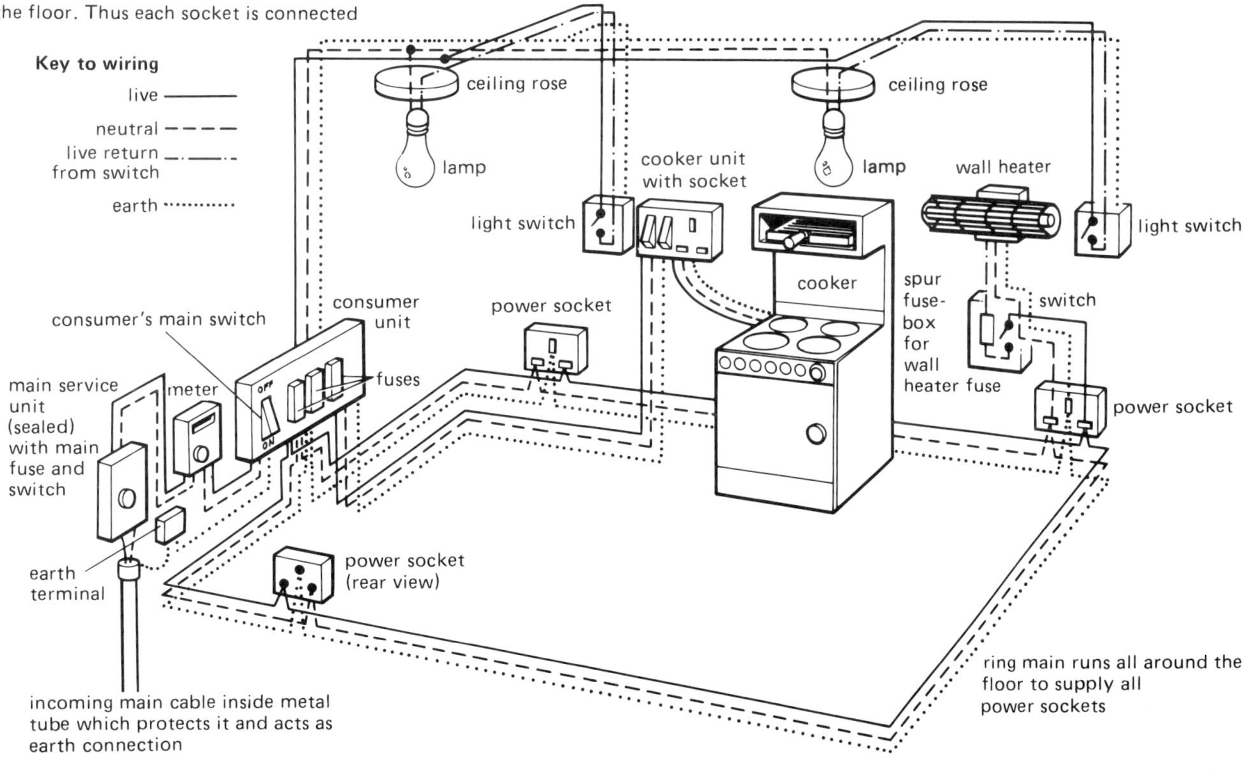

the neutral wire to touch a different part. So if you put one hand on each part, you would still get a shock. And the neutral wire would not actually be 'neutral' and safe. The appliance would contain two different dangerous wires.

Figure 8.9
Electric cables normally run vertically.

Figure 8.10
Electric cables may meander in the cavity of studded walls.

As it is, there is only one live wire. And the fact that it will send 240 V of electricity to earth, if it gets a chance, can be used to make appliances safer. The metal body of the appliance (for example, the casing of a refrigerator) is connected to earth. This is done not through the neutral wire but — for extra safety — with a special earth wire, which runs directly to earth in each home. At several points in the live wire (for example, inside the plug) there is a *fuse*, a thin piece of wire which will melt and break if a very large current flows through it.

Q 9
If the live wire comes loose inside a refrigerator and touches the casing, what will happen? (If it helps you to answer, draw a circuit diagram.)

Fuses are used only in the live wire, never in the neutral one. And in home wiring, switches are always installed in the live wire.

Q 10
Imagine that a switch is installed by mistake in the neutral wire of the power socket into which the refrigerator is plugged. This switch is off. The wiring inside the refrigerator is very bad. The earth wire breaks completely. The live wire comes loose and touches the casing. What could happen?

Q 11
If the socket were correctly wired, can you think of another mistake which could create the same danger?

House wiring is hidden under floors, behind skirting and inside walls. In walls, it runs straight up and down, for example down from the ceiling to a light switch, or up from the floor to a wall socket. Often you can work out where the wiring is. But you have to be very careful drilling holes in walls. If your drill touched the live wire of a buried cable, you can imagine the result. Never drill or nail into the wall straight above or below any electrical fitting.

Q 12
The cable used for house wiring is not like the flex used to connect appliances to plugs. Inside the outer casing of this cable, the earth wire is bare, without plastic sleeving. Why might this protect you if you hammered a nail into it?

TWO-WAY SWITCHING
Light switches are often arranged so that they can be turned on and off in two different places — for instance, at the top and bottom of the stairs. How does this work?

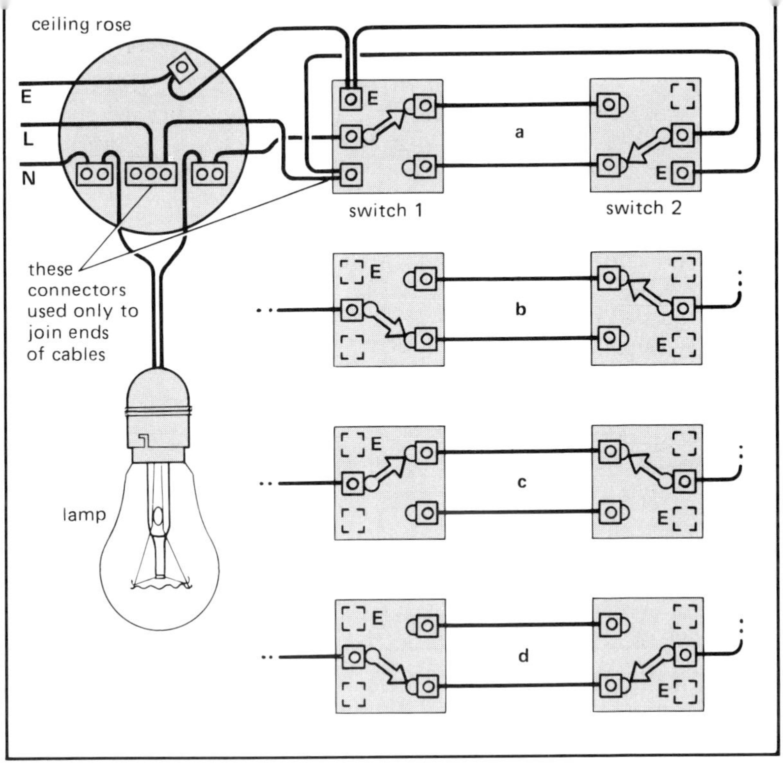

Figure 8.11

YOU WILL NEED:

Battery
Lamp in holder
2 crocodile clips
5 lengths of single flex
2 small wood blocks
6 drawing-pins
2 small metal strips
Wire strippers
Small screwdriver

1 Before you assemble the experiment, look at figure 8.11. This shows how a ceiling light is connected so that it can be turned on or off by either of two switches. Trace the flow of electricity from live (L) to neutral (N) in diagram *a*. With the switches in the position shown, would the light be on or off?

2 Answer the same question for diagrams *b*, *c* and *d*.

3 Inside the ceiling rose (the fitting on the ceiling from which the light hangs) and switch 1, there are several connectors where a wire goes in and comes straight out again without being connected to the lamp or the working part of the switch. On the live wire, this is just a way of joining the ends of the cables running to and from the rose and switch. But look at the earth wire connector in the two switches. A switch is set in a metal box in the wall, and the connector is in contact with the box. Why is this done?

4 The ceiling rose is made of plastic, and is not in a metal box. Why not?

5 Now you can make a model of a two-way switching system. It will use battery, not mains power. Mains electricity is not something to experiment with: it can easily kill you. ⚠

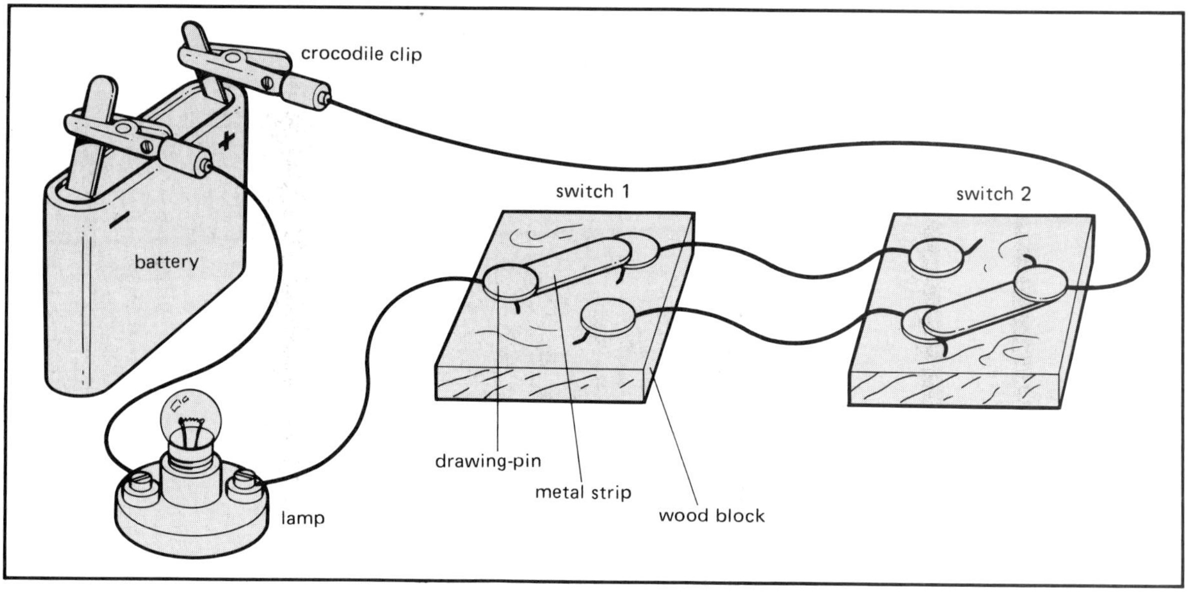

Figure 8.12

6 Use the wire strippers to remove 1 cm of insulation from the ends of all the wires. Twist the wire strands to stop them from spreading out.

7 Make the switches. Push a drawing pin through the hole in each metal strip and into a wood block. Don't push it right down yet. Press in the other drawing pins (not right down) so that the metal strip can move to touch either of them but not both at once.

8 Fit a crocodile clip to the ends of two of the pieces of flex. Loosen the screw, then wrap the bare end of the wire around it clockwise, under the washer if there is one. Tighten the screw.

9 Connect the rest of the circuit as in figure 8.12. Fit the wires to the screws on the lampholder as in step *8*. Clamp the bare ends of the other wires under the drawing pins by pressing the pins right down. Clip the crocodile clips to the battery terminals.

10 See which positions of the switches make the light go on and off.

11 Mains switches sometimes have a toggle which you move down for 'on' and up for 'off'. Sometimes they have a push-button that you just press, and the switch goes on if it's off, or off if it's on. Which type of switch would be better for a real two-way switching system in a house?

12 The model you made lacks some of the wiring of a real system. Why would there be no point in including this in the model?

8.6
HEATING THE HOME

In summer, houses are warmed by the sun, but in winter extra heat has to be supplied in Britain. The efficiency of the heating system and the fuel used determines comfort and cost.

Q 13
Find out what people mean by 'heat', and how it is transferred from one place to another.

Q 14
What factors determine the amount of heat needed to keep you comfortably warm in winter?

Q 15
Some rooms in the house are usually expected to be warmer than others. List the following rooms in order of the temperature that you think is required, starting with the room needing to be warmest: kitchen, living-room, bedroom, and bathroom. Give reasons for the order you chose.

What differences in temperature do you find in practice?

YOU WILL NEED:
Thermometers (several)

1 Using a thermometer and choosing the same time of day each time, record the temperature in a variety of rooms in the home. Alternatively, use classrooms and other rooms in school.

2 Try to account for the variations you discover.

Figure 8.13a
An old central heating boiler (about 1914). It had wide-bore pipes and gravity circulation; a large volume of water was needed, and this was not sensitive to controls.

Figure 8.13b
A modern wall-mounted gas central heating boiler.

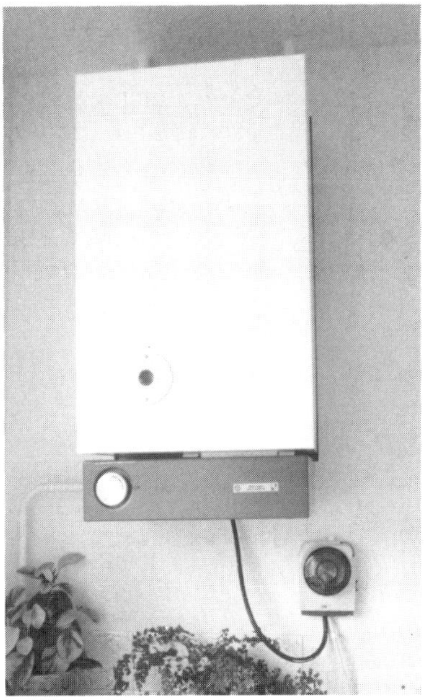

CENTRAL HEATING
This means heating the whole house from a central boiler or other energy source. The most common method of central heating is the wet system. A central boiler heats water which is circulated through the radiators in each room. A second set of pipes carries hot water for washing purposes. An alternative method uses ducted warm air for the space-heating part of the system.

Q 16
What are the advantages and disadvantages of ducted air systems?

Worksheet PM11 tells you more about central heating. The central boiler can run on gas, coal, oil, or electricity. The most common energy source in Britain is gas (72 per cent in 1984).

Q 17
Why do you think gas is so popular?

Q 18
Given that you have fitted central heating in your home, what other factors should you consider in order to obtain value for money?

8.7
USING FUEL EFFICIENTLY
The finite nature of fossil fuels, increasing costs of exploration and recovery, and technological research into alternative energy sources are all factors contributing to higher fuel costs. Reducing energy consumption in the home is not only good for your pocket; it also benefits the country and indeed the whole World.

The motto 'heat your home and not the street outside' makes a lot of sense.

Find out whether heat passes through walls.

YOU WILL NEED:

Thermometers (several)

1 Record the temperature on the other side of the wall from a radiator.

2 Compare it with other parts of the same room.

Q 19

Not all types of houses lose heat at the same rate. Put the following types of houses in order of rate of heat loss, starting with the highest and ending with the lowest. (Assume that each house is of identical shape and size, and has the same level of insulation.)

a semi-detached
b detached
c centre of a row of terraced houses.

Figure 8.14
Traditional open fires are not very efficient. (This photograph shows the chainmaker's cottage in the Black Country Museum.)

HEAT LOSS AND INSULATION

Building materials and methods of construction vary in their ability to transmit heat. Some transmit heat quickly, others more slowly. Rates of heat energy loss through different building materials and constructions are calculated as U values. This represents rate of heat loss measured in watts per square metre per degree centigrade temperature difference ($W/m^2/^\circ C$).

A small U value means that heat conductance is low. A small U value therefore means that only a small amount of heat is lost from the house.

Q 20

Brick walls have different U values depending on their construction. Calculate the rates of heat loss in watts through each of two types of wall from the data at the top of the next page, using the formula:

U value X area X temperature difference = wattage

Structure	U value with no insulation	Insulated as follows	U value with insulation
External walls (cavity construction):			
Brick both layers	1.6	with cavity insulation	0.5
Brick outside block inside	1.0	with cavity insulation	0.4
Roofs (pitched construction):	2.7	with 50 mm loft insulation	0.6
		with 100 mm loft insulation	0.35
		with 200 mm loft insulation	0.2
Windows (single-glazed):			
Metal-framed	5.6	double-glazed	3.7
Wood-framed	4.0	double-glazed	2.5

a Solid brick wall (two bricks thick) with a U value of 2.1
b Cavity brick wall (both layers brick) with a U value of 1.6

Area of each wall: 12 m^2
Internal house temperature: 20°C
External temperature: 10°C

As you can see from table 8.2, walls, roof, and windows have different U values. Together they are responsible for about 80 per cent of total heat loss. The remaining 20 per cent escapes through ventilators and gaps around doors and windows.

Figure 8.15
Fibreglass insulation being unrolled between the joists of the attic.

Q 21
Look at table 8.2.
a Compare the U value of a roof with and without insulation. Is it worth insulating the loft?
b Now consider double-glazing. Is this effective?

Insulation can save fuel and make home heating less expensive. However, the householder has to decide if the cost of insulation will be repaid by the savings made.

Q 22
a Now try to think of all the less obvious ways in which fuel can be saved in the home. (Exclude insulation of lofts, cavity walls, and double-glazing since these have been dealt with already.)
b Which of your ideas could be carried out by householders themselves?

BACKGROUND READING

WHY IS GAS A POPULAR FUEL?

Only thirty years ago the British gas industry was on its knees. Over 1000 separate manufacturing works supplied gas to a dwindling market. Gas was regarded as dirty, smelly, dangerous, expensive — and old fashioned. In the domestic and premium fuel markets electricity with its clean, modern image held sway.

Today gas is the most popular fuel in the homes of Britain and is increasingly used by industry and commerce. British Gas, the nationalized undertaking which eventually grew out of the amalgamation of the many private undertakings of the pre-war period, is now the largest fully integrated gas industry in the world and among the ten largest businesses of any kind in Britain. The image of gas has also been transformed — it is now seen by its customers as a modern, safe, easily controllable fuel which is also excellent value for money.

This change around is not due to a public relations exercise. It is a result of two technological revolutions. The first saw gas being made from oil, instead of coal, and the import of liquefied natural gas from Algeria. The second was the momentous discovery in the late 1960s that enormous reserves of natural gas lay beneath the North Sea. The story of how this discovery was exploited so that gas could be piped into Britain's homes and factories involves human endeavour and technological ingenuity of a high order. In addition to the enormous expense

Table 8.2
U values of walls, roofs, and windows.

of North Sea exploration, the project meant the creation of an entirely new pipeline network and the conversion of many millions of homes and factories from the old town gas.

The vital link in the chain which binds North Sea production to homes throughout Britain is of course the network of pipelines which deliver gas quietly, quickly, and unobtrusively to cities, towns, and villages. Now over 80 per cent of the population has access to a piped gas supply.

Like all fossil fuels natural gas is a finite resource. However, research has been going on since the 1950s to find an artificial means of producing the same kind of gas. This research effort goes on, so that when natural gas eventually runs out, perhaps some time in the 21st century, an efficient substitute will have been found and developed to ensure that Britain's gas consumers will still be able to buy the fuel they prefer.

Figure 8.16
A mobile production platform in shallow water off the Dorset coast. The platform moves up and down on its four 'legs' according to the depth of water in which it is operating. The drilling rig is the tower on the lefthand side.

Figure 8.17
During transmission the pressure of the gas — which is what keeps it flowing — needs to be boosted from time to time. This is accomplished in a series of compressor stations along the network which are powered by enormous engines like this Rolls Royce RB211 jet aircraft engine.

Figure 8.18
The national transmission system of British Gas is almost 5000 km long. Underground pipes carry gas at high pressure from the far north-east right down to the south-west coast of Britain. Underground transmission means speedy restoration of land to usefulness, and a pollution-free (both visually and chemically) system of distribution.

CHAPTER 9

Stopping the rot

Figure 9.1
Building a house — a large input of materials and energy.

Figure 9.2
Houses decay if they are not properly maintained.

Our homes and the furnishings they contain may be attractive and satisfying when they are new, but will not stay that way for long unless they are maintained and repaired. A house or flat represents a big financial commitment, and will only keep its value if it is kept in good order.

In Chapters 7 and 8 you learned about house structure and about how energy supplies add to the comfort of the home and help to lessen the human energy needed for its maintenance. This chapter will help you to assess the seriousness of any problems of home maintenance that may arise. You will learn more about what is likely to go wrong, what can be done about it by people living in the house, and what is firmly in the sphere of the professional.

9.1 USE OF SPACE

Organization and order keep cleaning and maintenance to a minimum, avoid frustration, and reduce the probability of accidents. Figure 9.3 shows how household things can be kept off the floor to make cleaning easier.

Careful and thoughtful planning is also needed to make maximum use of available space. Built-in furniture is common in bedrooms and kitchens.

Figure 9.3
Keeping things off the ground makes cleaning easier.

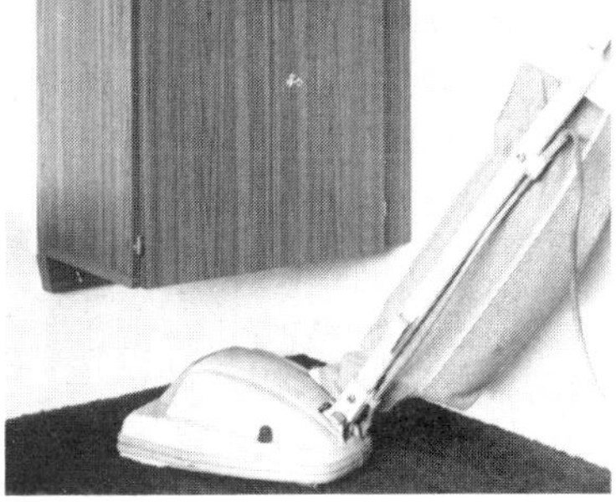

Q 1
Would you choose to have built-in furniture in your home? Give reasons for and against.

9.2
REPLACING AND ADJUSTING

It pays to make your own replacements and adjustments if possible. Unfortunately, many modern household appliances are very complex and the needs of cheap mass production make it difficult or impossible for the amateur to dismantle them. Often the cause of a machine's failure may be very simple, as in the case of a blocked filter in the water inlet pipe of a washing-machine. This is when the instruction booklet is needed so keep them to hand. If a specialist has to be called in, you will need practical intelligence to describe the fault accurately. It is all too easy to mislead visiting engineers so that they bring the wrong spare parts. Visits cost money! If the cost of a repair is likely to exceed 50 per cent of the price of replacing an ageing machine it might be best to buy a new one.

Figure 9.4
Tiles may come loose and need sticking down again.

Specific instruction books are not available for dealing with faults in simpler appliances such as water taps and doors that bind. For these types of replacement or adjustment a small library of DIY books is necessary.

ELECTRICAL EQUIPMENT

Electrical gadgets and equipment often need repair and replacement.

Q 2
Before adjusting, cleaning, or investigating the failure of any electrical appliance, what golden rule should be followed?

One of the commonest replacements is that of electrical fuses. Although fuses may fail due to age there is usually a more specific reason. You can see if a wired fuse has burned out. This is not so with cartridge fuses, so it is a good idea to check if they have really blown or not. An appliance may appear to have failed because some other gadget on the same circuit has fused the entire circuit. Alternatively, there might be a power cut! Very occasionally even a brand new replacement fuse may be faulty.

Q 3
a What causes of a fuse blowing can you think of?
b How would you test a cartridge fuse for continuity?
c What factors determine the size of fuse that you would use for a replacement?

If the insulation on the supply flex of an appliance is worn, it should be replaced completely rather than repaired with insulating tape.

Q 4
What points should be considered when choosing a replacement flex?

Lamp bulbs are labelled according to their wattage. Bulbs of various wattages should be kept in store, as shops are seldom open when they fail.

Q 5
Would a 100-watt bulb give more or less light than a 40-watt one?

Q 6
What factors determine the size and type of the replacement bulb that you select for a particular light fitting?

Q 7
If, after replacing a bulb of a plug-in table lamp it still doesn't light, what would you do?

Q 8
An electric fan heater will not work when you switch it on. The cartridge fuse in the plug and the wiring appear to be in good order. What would you try next?

PLUMBING AND CENTRAL HEATING

The water supply system of a house is another area in which replacements and adjustments are necessary at fairly frequent intervals.

Q 9
Write down as many examples of where these might occur as you can think of. For each one, state whether you think you could deal with it yourself.

A wet central heating system carries water and may need adjustments from time to time. Sometimes, when the central heating programmer is set to heating radiators and the boiler is functioning normally, the radiators do not heat up. Another trick that they can play is for most of them to work while one or two remain cold.

Figure 9.5
Bleeding a radiator.

Q 10
a What are the most probable reasons for none of the radiators working?
b Why might one or two radiators not work? What would you do to correct the fault?

Other water blockages involve waste pipes from baths and washbasins.

Q 11
How would you unblock them?

Freezing can also result in blockages in waste pipes.

Q 12
a Apart from extreme cold, what causes bath and washbasin wastes to freeze? What can be done to prevent it?
b Why does water freezing in pipes cause joints to open or pipes to split?
c What action would you take if a water pipe is blocked due to freezing?
d How would you cope with any burst that might result?

DOORS, WINDOWS, LOCKS, AND DRAWERS

Wooden doors and hinged window frames often start to bind. This means that they catch on the frame and refuse to close. The obvious solution is to shave off some wood, but this is not always the answer.

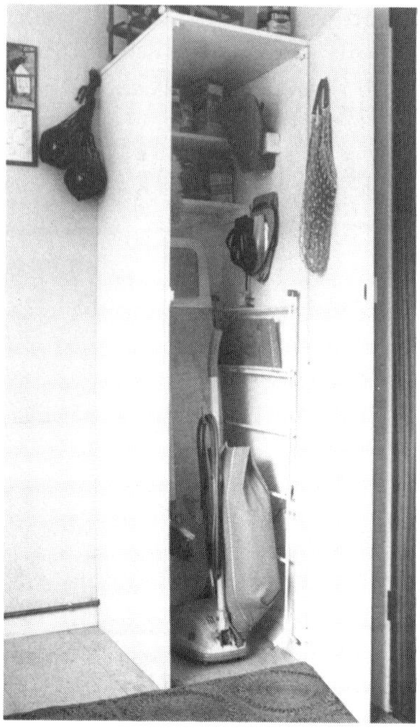

Q 13

What reasons for a door binding can you think of? Illustrate your answers with clear diagrams.

Q 14

There are many different designs of drawer. If the sliders are made of wood and it is stiff to operate, how would you cure it?

Q 15

Door locks may be hard to turn and there are several reasons why this might be so. What reasons can you think of, and what cures would you propose?

The list of adjustments and minor replacements that are continuously needed to keep a home functioning properly is endless. This section can only give some of the more common examples.

9.3
FIXING

Hanging pictures, putting up shelves and coat-hooks, assembling kitchen cupboards, repairing china, and sticking down laminates onto work surfaces are all examples of an endless list of fixing one thing to another. Man-made boards such as hardboard, chipboard and blockboard have replaced natural wood to a considerable extent. In addition, plastics of different sorts are now in widespread use. This bewildering variety of materials and construction methods has resulted in an explosion of mechanical and chemical fixing agents. To get it right first time, look it up in a DIY book. Think before you fix!

Figure 9.7
Small shelves supported by plastic screw-in pieces.

Figure 9.8
Sagging shelf.

The three chief methods of fixing things involve the use of nails, screws, or glues. Sometimes, for extra strength, glue is used in addition to screws or nails.

Q 16

a List the advantages and disadvantages in the use of screws and nails.

b Now list the advantages and disadvantages of using adhesives as opposed to the use of nails and screws.

There are more than twenty different types of nails, many of which are designed for a particular function. For best results you should use the right kind of nail for the job.

Q 17

Draw the shape of nail you would use for:

a securing the fabric to a chair
b making a picture frame
c making a go-cart.

In each case, explain your choice.

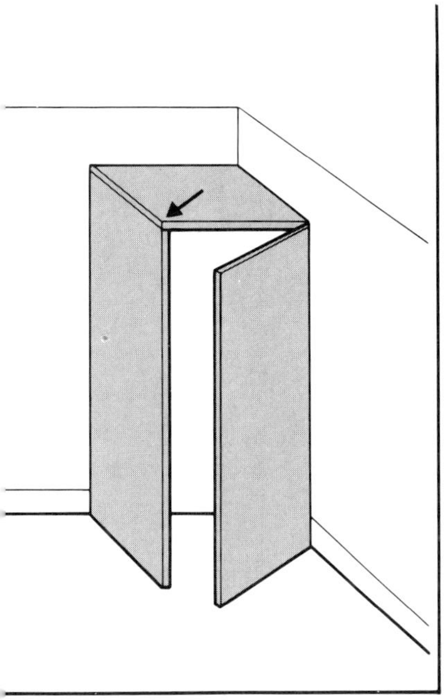

Figure 9.6
Broom cupboard made of three pieces of chipboard.

Chipboard is a man-made board made by compressing resin-coated particles of wood by heat and pressure. Although veneered versions are used extensively for kitchen furniture in particular, normal screws will not grip in this material for any length of time. Figure 9.6 shows a broom cupboard made from three pieces of plastic-covered chipboard built into the corner of a kitchen.

Q 18
What methods of fixing are possible for the butt joint arrowed in the diagram?

Q 19
Because modern internal doors are usually hollow, it is difficult to fix towel-rails and clothes-hooks to them. How can this problem be overcome?

Q 20
Special fixings are also required when attaching wall cupboards and shelf brackets to masonry walls. List the tools and materials required for driving screws into solid walls.

Q 21
Before drilling a hole in a wall, what precautions should you take? (See figures 8.9 and 8.10 on page 64.)

Figure 9.9
Removing hard water scaling from a shower thermostat.

Q 22
Kitchen wall cupboards can be heavy, and more so when filled with crockery. The fixing holes on the back may not be sufficient to make an absolutely safe job. What additional support is advisable?

Q 23
Another job requiring wall fixing is the erection of shelves. Traditional shelf brackets have one arm longer than the other. Which arm should be fixed to the wall? Why?

Q 24
What is wrong with the shelf shown in figure 9.8? How could this have been avoided?

Q 25
Another common fixing job is that of hanging pictures. How do you decide on the exact height and position? What would you do to fix it?

9.4 KEEPING OUT OF TROUBLE

In Chapters 7 and 8 we looked at house structure and essential services. This section deals with the recognition of faults so that they can be checked before they get too serious. Since prevention is better than cure, the same knowledge can be applied to seeing that problems are never allowed to start in the first place. Lack of simple maintenance like failing to clean out a gutter can be the first step into trouble. Thoughtless actions on our part, such as bridging the damp-proof course with garden soil, can also lead to difficulties.

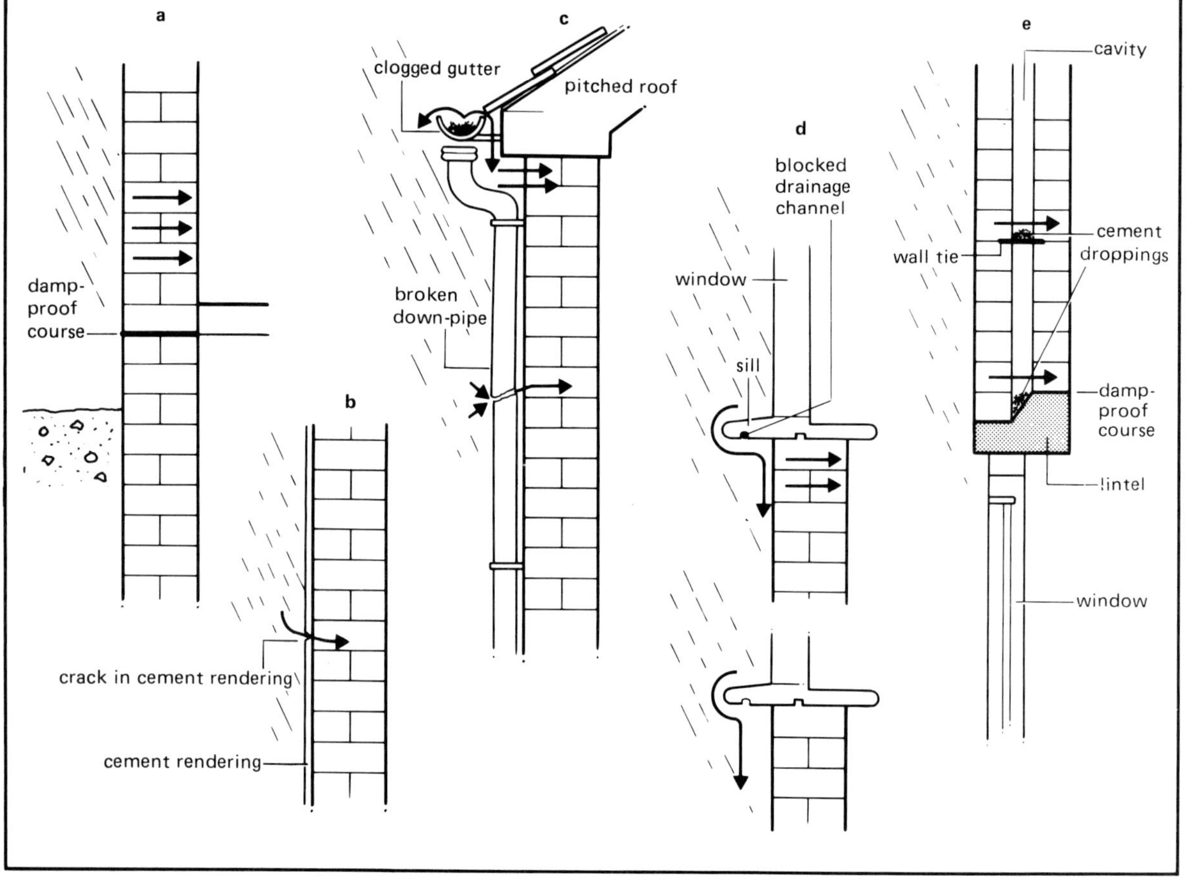

Figure 9.10
How damp can get in.

DAMP

One of the commonest household problems is damp. The first step towards prevention or cure is to recognize the cause or causes. The three chief causes are as follows, but it is not always easy to distinguish between them.

Penetrating damp: water penetrating external walls from the outside and soaking through.

Rising damp: water rising up the walls from the ground beneath.

Condensation: the condensation of moisture onto cold surfaces from air laden with water vapour. (Remember what happens if you breathe onto a cold window-pane or spectacle lens.)

Q 26

From your knowledge of house structure (Chapter 7) and by studying the drawings in figure 9.10, list the various reasons why rain might penetrate the outer walls of a house.

Even if external walls are sound and waterproof they might still become damp. This would show as damp patches edged by a salt deposit at the base of and on the inside of ground floor walls. Bricks are fairly porous and water can rise through them by capillary action. Fortunately, cement-based mortar between them acts as a barrier. This is not true of the lime and sand mortars found in older houses.

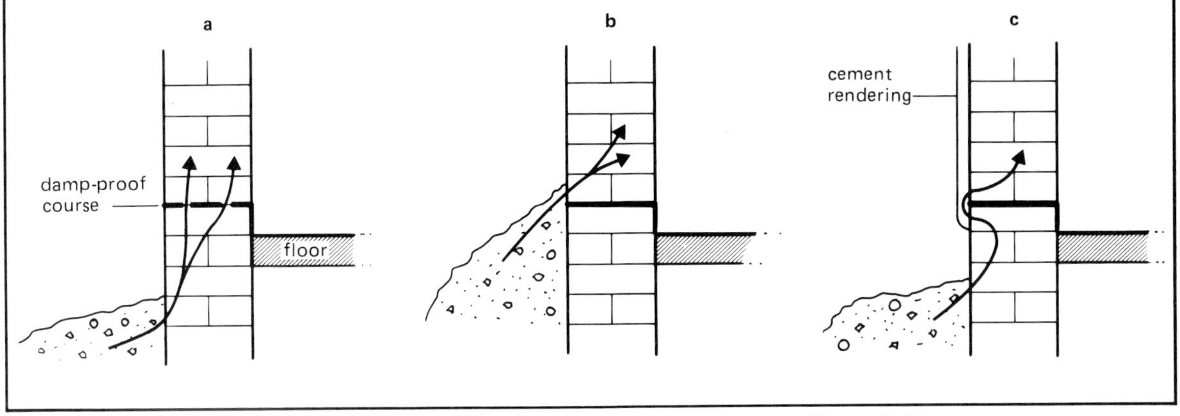

Figure 9.11
How rising damp can get in.

Q 27
List as many causes as you can of rising damp. Figure 9.11 will help you.

Q 28
a Why do you think air moisture levels vary from room to room and from season to season?
b Which areas of the house are most likely to be damp?
c What do you think can be done to reduce condensation?

LAGGING

The most effective way of conserving heat in a house is to insulate the floor of the loft. However, this has consequences for the loft and the roof.

Q 29
a How does loft insulation affect the temperature of the loft space?
b What effect will this have on water-pipes and cisterns in the loft?
c How would you try to prevent the problems that might result?

Lagging is often carried well up into the eaves, reducing ventilation, and air gaps are left around pipes entering from below and around trap-doors, allowing warm moist air to rise up into the loft.

Q 30
What would be the result of this?

Reduced ventilation and low temperatures in loft spaces, together with the leakage of warm moist air from below, can result in condensation onto the wooden roofing struts. This means that fungus can grow, including the types of fungi that produce wet rot and dry rot.

Both fungi produce threads which digest the wood they are growing upon. The several different types of fungi responsible for wet rot cannot spread further than the moist area. Dry rot needs much less moisture and can penetrate masonry walls seeking further supplies of moist timber. This is the most dangerous disease of wood. It is characterized by dry brick-shaped surface cracks. The only remedy is complete replacement

Figure 9.12
Loft and cistern insulation (this can be damaged by mice, as in this picture).

Figure 9.13
This simple experiment shows how rot starts. Two pieces of bread were left under separate tumblers for four days. The left one was dampened and mould has grown; the right one was dry and no mould has grown.

of the wood. Eventually, as is typical of fungi, both types develop fruiting bodies which produce air-borne spores for dissemination throughout the house.

Q 31
What could be done to help prevent wet rot and dry rot?

Figure 9.14
A rotting window-frame: regular painting would have prevented this.

PAINTING
External wood can also rot if it is not protected by paint. Minute cracks in this surface skin will allow water to penetrate to the wood beneath.

Experiment with painting different materials for yourself.

YOU WILL NEED:

Pieces of:
wood, bare
wood, primed and undercoated
metal, bare
metal, primed
rough concrete or breezeblock
plasterboard

Paints:
emulsion
interior gloss
exterior gloss
exterior stone paint

Brush
Jar of white spirit
Sink
Newspaper
Rags
Pieces of old painted wood, metal, and plaster

1 You have four different materials. Imagine that the wood is the outside of a front door. The metal is a fitting inside the house. The concrete is part of the outside wall. The plasterboard is part of the wall of a room. You also have four kinds of paint. Which are you going to use for each? Write this down and show your teacher before you start painting.

2 First paint the bare wood. What happens to the paint? If you let the paint dry and put on another coat of paint, or maybe several more, how would the result look? In real life, other kinds of paint are used for the lower coats. Why? Can you guess the difference between primer and undercoat?

3 Paint the primed and undercoated wood. Try to use as little paint as possible to cover the surface completely. How do you handle the brush to achieve this?

4 Find out what to use to clean the brush when using this kind of paint. Clean it thoroughly, then dry it on the rag.

5 Now paint the bare metal, and then the primed metal. What difference do you notice in the result? If you put the paint on very thickly, what happens? If a piece of painted steel was to be used in a damp place, what difference would it make if it had not been primed before painting?

6 Find out what to use to clean the brush when using this kind of paint. Clean it thoroughly, then dry it on the rag.

7 Now paint the concrete. You will notice that it is quite difficult to cover it completely without leaving little gaps, because of the rough surface, unless you use a wasteful amount of paint. Why must the surface be completely covered? How do you handle the brush to achieve this?

8 Find out what to use to clean the brush when using this kind of paint. Clean it thoroughly, then dry it on the rag.

9 Now paint the plasterboard. Is one coat enough to cover it? If not, let it dry for 10 minutes, then put on a second coat. If painting a real wall, what would you do?

10 Find out what to use to clean the brush when using this kind of paint. Clean it thoroughly, then dry it on the rag.

11 Stone paint contains real stone, finely powdered. Why?

12 Look at the samples of old painted wood, metal, and plaster. Can you tell what kinds of paint have been used? What has happened to it? Would you say that any samples had been badly painted?

Figure 9.15
Pest control.

RUST

The widespread use of plastics in house structure and services makes rust much less of a problem than it used to be.

Q 32
Which areas are likely to be vulnerable to rust? What should you do to prevent it? How would you deal with it if it occurs?

PEST CONTROL

Wood may be attacked internally by insects (woodworm).

Q 33
a Which stage of the life cycle of the woodworm does the damage?
b How can damage by woodworm be avoided?
c What would you do if it happened?

Masonry wasps burrow in sand, and may also weaken walls by burrowing into the soft mortar between bricks to make their nests. There are other insect pests in Britain which do no structural harm but may carry disease. The house-fly is the most important of these.

Q 34
Why is the house-fly a hazard to health? What can be done to prevent it from spreading disease?

Mice and rats may do structural damage, but can be more dangerous from the point of view of hygiene.

Q 35
How can these pests best be avoided, or eliminated if they come?

BACKGROUND READING

DO IT YOURSELF: PAINTING AND DECORATING

Julia McSwiney spent eighteen months working as a painter-decorator. Here is her account of what the work involves.

My interest in decorating began when I first painted my own room. Later I became apprenticed to a painter and decorator. My only qualifications were enthusiasm and the ability to handle a paint-brush competently. As with most building trades, the best way to learn is to work for someone who teaches you on the job.

Figure 9.16
A painter at work.

You can do painting and decorating yourself. It can be great fun and saves a lot of money. Don't be overawed and don't hurry. Read all the manufacturers' instructions carefully before beginning. Remove curtains and light furniture, put heavy items in the middle of the room and protect these and the carpets. Wear old clothing and shoes — you *will* get paint on you! Keep rooms well ventilated.

Preparation is essential. The ceiling and walls should be smooth and washed with water. Sand the woodwork down and scrape down any very damaged paintwork using paint stripper. Bare wood needs treating. Holes must be filled with putty and knots dabbed with patent knotting before applying a primer. The woodwork is painted after the walls (non-drip gloss is easiest).

Score old wallpaper with a scraper, soak it using sponges, scrape it off, and wash down to remove old paste. Plaster large holes, fill small ones with Polyfilla. If the walls are very bumpy you should hang lining paper, allow it to dry, then paint it. This is a good way to learn papering, as lining paper is cheap, has no pattern and some types, like 'woodchip', cover up many imperfections.

Paint the ceiling first. White is good for low ceilings. A high ceiling will seem lower if you paint it a shade darker than the walls. When covering a darker with a lighter colour, first paint one coat of cheaper white emulsion. Use two coats of your final colour and don't skimp on the amount. Light affects colour. A strong colour may look exciting in a large, sunny room but too oppressive in a small, windowless room.

Essential tools are a bucket, sponge, scraper, and at least three good brushes: 100-mm for walls and two 40-mm, one for primer, undercoat, and gloss (clean with white spirit) and one for emulsion (clean with water). A 20-mm brush (called a fitch) is ideal for fiddly jobs like windows. You may prefer a roller and tray but you will still need a brush to paint corners and edges.

Initially keep ideas simple and within your budget and if you think you can tackle a problem, go ahead. Experiment with small pots of paint and good luck. You can create a happy home from an empty shell.

CHAPTER 10

Ergonomics and efficiency

10.1 ERGONOMICS IN THE HOME

Ergonomics is the study of people in their environment. It is concerned with the *interaction* between people and the things around them — that is, the effect that people and things have on each other.

The main aim of ergonomics is to try to arrange 'the world' so that it fits people the way they are, rather than trying to make people adapt to 'the world'. For the purposes of this book, 'the world' we are considering is home. In each activity people interact with things — the architectural features, the furniture, and the equipment in the home.

Figure 10.1
Equipment should fit people the way they are.

Figure 10.2
Luggage trolleys at Heathrow — designing 'the world' to meet people's needs.

Q 1
List the things with which people interact in homes. Try to fit them into categories.

10.2
THE HOME AS A 'SYSTEM'

Ergonomists look at people and things together; that is, they think of their interaction as a *system*. So, for example, the home and the people in it constitute a system. Shelter, heat, light, ventilation, and equipment are provided in the home so that people are able to eat, sleep, wash, and relax. The purpose of this system is to allow people to act efficiently, safely, and in comfort.

Q 2
Make a list of other systems that you can think of, and describe them.

Figure 10.3
Which method of cleaning carpets is most efficient?

10.3
HOME AS A WORK-PLACE

Many of the home activities such as washing, cleaning, and cooking demand physical and mental effort. Someone doing housework uses about the same amount of energy as someone doing a light industrial job. In many homes nowadays everyone goes out to work, and they have little time to spend on housework. One of the concerns of domestic ergonomics is to calculate how housework could be done with less effort and more efficiency.

Over the years, advances in technology have produced labour-saving devices for the home. However, this equipment is still used by people, and its design must take into account what they can do.

Q 3
What activities do you consider are included in housework?

Q 4
What labour-saving devices are now in common use?

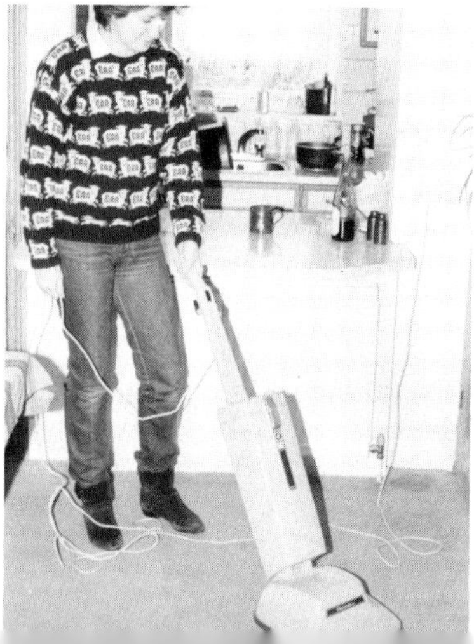

10.4
DESIGN FOR FUNCTION

An important factor which the designer has to consider is the *function* — or purpose — of whatever is being designed. In section 10.2 you looked at the overall purpose of the home as a system. However, within this general system there are many smaller systems in operation, each having their own particular function. For example, a person and a vacuum-cleaner together constitute a system whose function is to clean carpets. This is much more efficient than a person with a dustpan and brush, particularly if the person has a bad back!

A more complicated example is a food preparation system. The elements of this are food, the equipment and the person carrying

Figure 10.4
The home as a system.

Figure 10.5
The design of equipment should take people's abilities into account.

Figure 10.7
People are not all the same size.

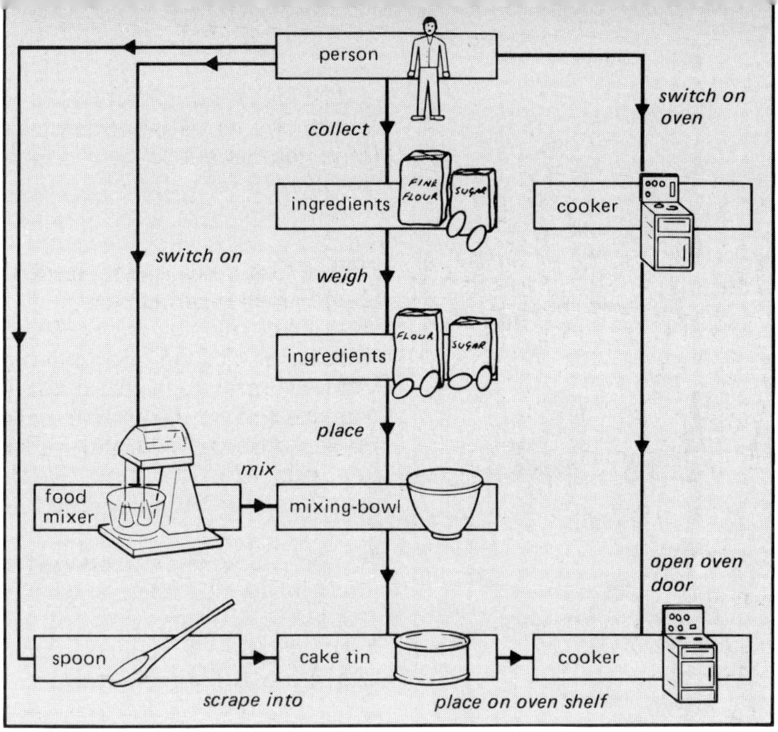

Figure 10.6
The interaction of different components of a system.

out the task. Making a cake might require the system shown in figure 10.6. You can see from a diagram like this where the interactions between components of the system occur.

Q 5
Study figure 10.6. Using the information you have learned in this chapter, describe the most important factors which influence the effective interaction between the person, the ingredients, and the equipment.

Q 6
Prepare a similar chart to explain the system for another household task.

Although people often adapt equipment or tools, and use them outside the system for which they were designed, it is never as efficient, safe, or comfortable as using the proper system. For example, when you use a nailfile as a screwdriver, eat a meal in an armchair, or stand on a chair to change a light-bulb, you are operating outside the proper system.

Q 7
Suggest three other examples of how we adapt equipment and use it outside its own system. For each one, say how efficient and how safe it is.

10.5 DESIGN FOR PEOPLE

People, of course, are not all exactly the same. They differ in size, shape, strength, and mental abilities, as well as in many other ways. These variations must be taken into account when designing homes and the equipment they contain.

DESIGN INFORMATION

First, we could start by looking at the physical differences between people. It is a common observation that people come in all different shapes and sizes. If you are designing a piece of equipment, how do you allow for these differences?

The differences between individuals can be classified in various ways. For instance, you can describe an individual in terms of his or her physical measurements. The science of body measurements is called *anthropometry*. Figure 10.9 shows some dimensions which are often measured. If we take one of these dimensions — stature (or height), for example — and measure a large number of people, we find that there are a few people who are very short, a few people who are very tall, and a large number of people who fall between these extremes.

In fact, if we measure a sufficiently large number of people, the *distribution* of their stature when plotted on graph paper is a 'bell-shaped' curve, as you can see in figure 10.10. Most linear (straight-line) dimensions of the body have similar distributions when plotted on a graph.

In order to get a curve as smooth as this you will need to measure a great many people. You may, however, obtain the same general shape with the measurements of your class.

Figure 10.8

YOU WILL NEED:

- Steel tape measure
- Ruler
- Paper
- Pencil
- Sellotape

Figure 10.9
Common anthropometric dimensions.

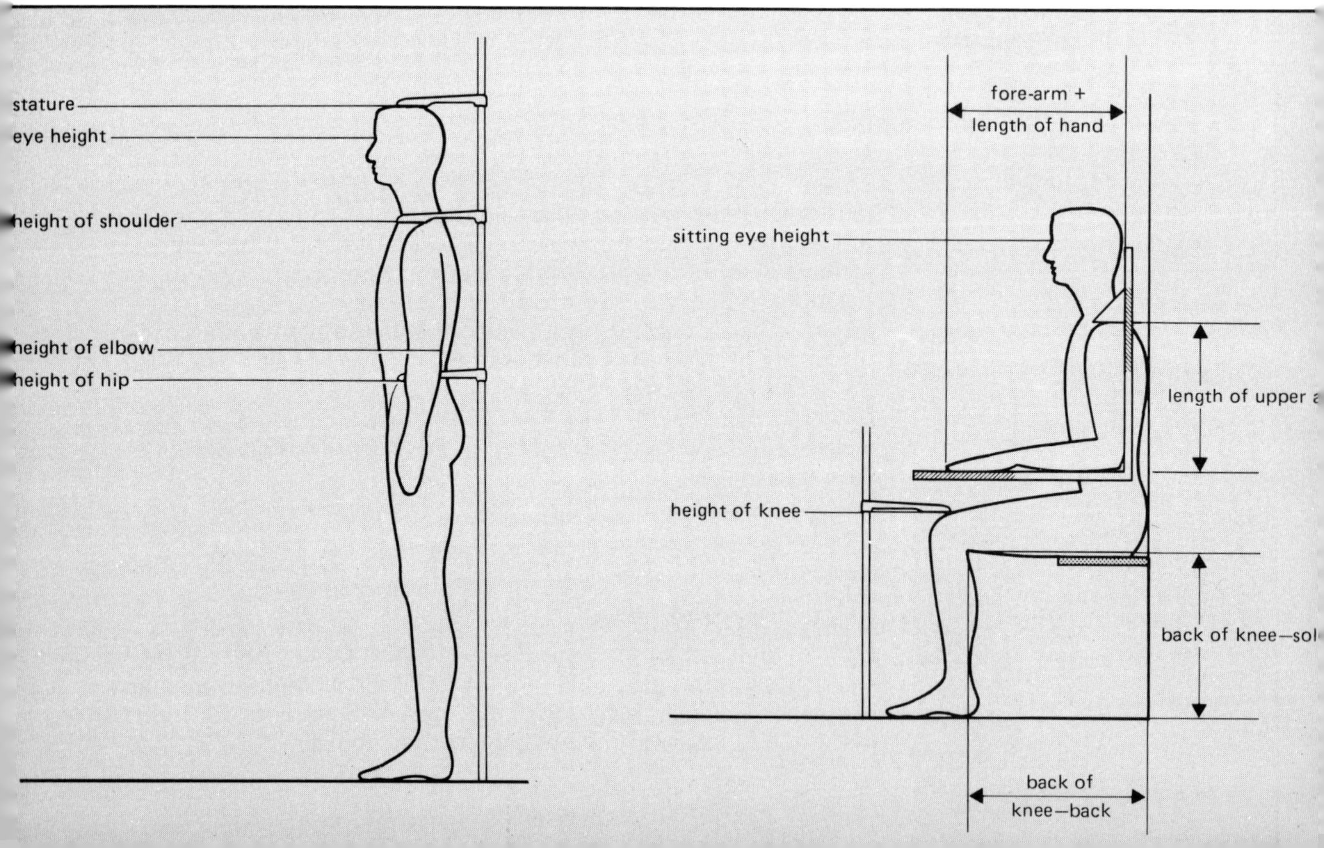

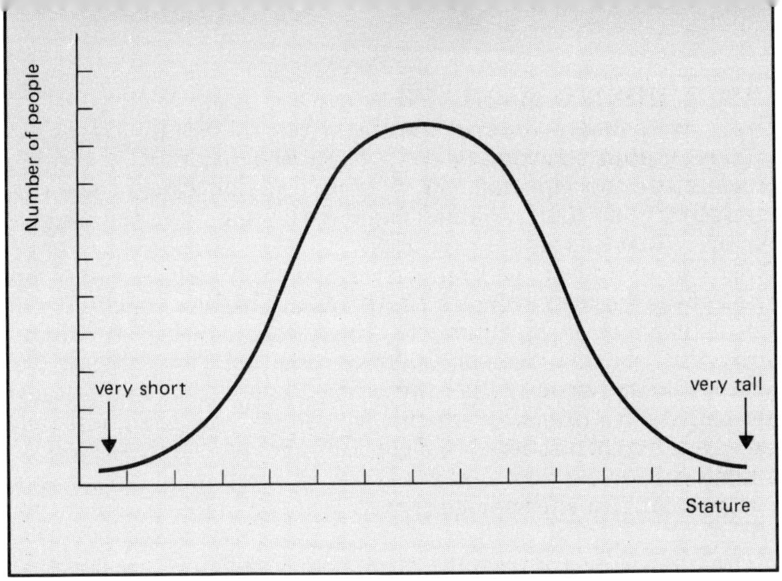

Figure 10.10

1 Attach the paper to the wall with Sellotape at about head height.

2 Ask each member of the class to stand against the wall (first telling them to remove their shoes).

Q 8
Why do you think it is important to get them to take off their shoes?

3 Rest the ruler on top of their head, parallel to the floor, and mark off their height on the paper.

4 Measure the distance from the floor to the mark you have just made, using the steel tape measure.

5 Put the results in a table.

6 Using the information from your table, draw two charts, one for girls, one for boys, similar to the one shown in figure 10.11.

Q 9
What differences are there between the girls' chart and the boys' chart?

Figure 10.11

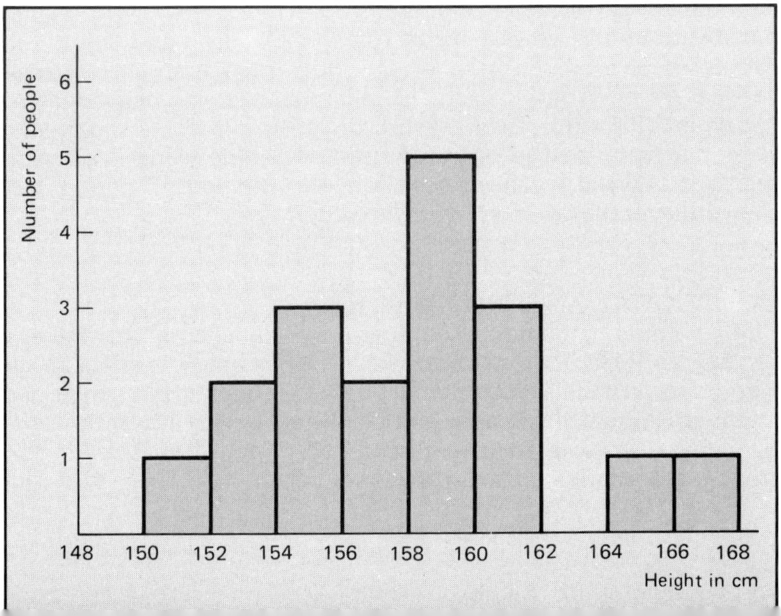

RANGE, SPREAD, AVERAGE

You have seen how human body size can be described by a set of curves, each referring to a different dimension. How can the designer use this information? If you have not thought about it carefully, your first response might be to say, 'use the average person'. What happens if you do?

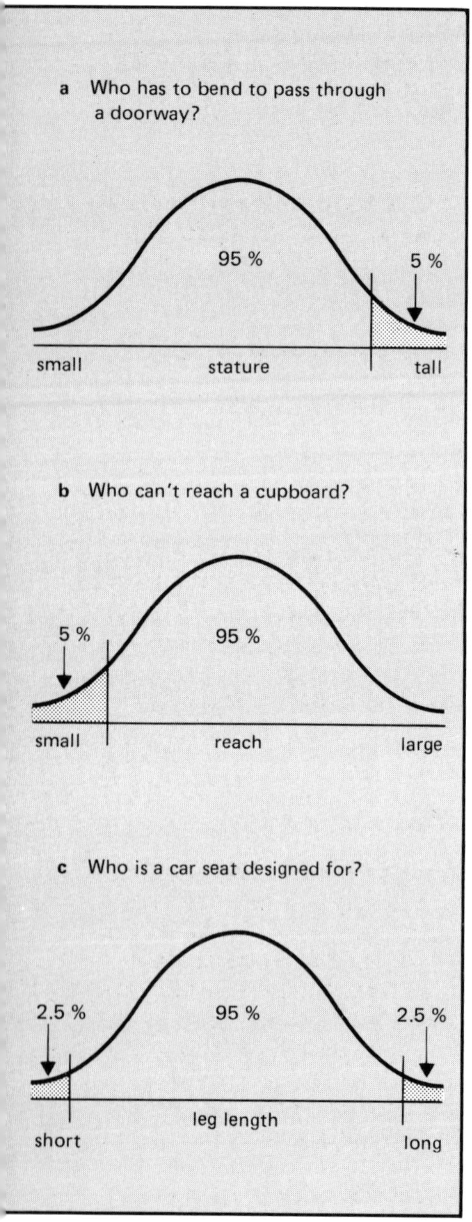

Figure 10.12

Look at the diagram in figure 10.10 again. The line which divides the distribution in half indicates the average stature. By definition, the average person is taller than 50 per cent of the population and shorter than the other 50 per cent. If you design the height of a doorway for the average person, half the people will have to bend down to get through it! There would be similar difficulties with any object or equipment which was designed just for the average person.

If designing for the average is incorrect, what is the answer? Using the doorway example, if you don't want *anyone* to bang their head, you should obviously design it for the tallest person in the population. However, there are difficulties with this too. As you move towards the end of the curve in figure 10.10, there are progressively fewer people, until you come right to the end, which will be the tallest person.

Is it economical, sensible, or practical to alter the design of houses and to use extra materials just to accommodate the few people who are very, very tall? The answer, of course, must be no. What the designer has to do is to decide what percentage of the population it is economical to accommodate. In other words, he will design for a range of people. This range will contain the majority of the people; those who fall outside the range will be inconvenienced, to a greater or lesser degree.

LARGE OR SMALL?

Clearly, in the doorway example the aim would be to include all but the tallest people. For other objects you would be concerned with the opposite end of the distribution. For example, if you were to design storage cupboards for the kitchen, you should decide upon the height above the work surface and the depth of the shelves on the basis of the individuals with the *shortest* vertical or horizontal reach. In fact, the size and placement of many architectural fittings and furniture should be designed with reference to the range of sizes of people using the equipment. It is usual to choose the range to include 95 per cent of the adult population for any given dimension.

FUNCTIONAL ANTHROPOMETRY

The example of storage cupboards given above illustrates a further important point. Knowledge of people's vertical reach can only provide very general guidelines about how high the cupboard should be. People cannot always simply reach upwards as high as possible to a cupboard; they are often standing in front of a work surface and must reach into the cupboard,

Figure 10.13

Figure 10.14

perhaps reading the label on a particular item before selecting and grasping it. For this type of task a more realistic method of measuring the space required is necessary.

This is called *functional anthropometry*. The idea is to measure the space required when actually performing the task. The people used in such a study would be selected so that small, medium and large sizes were included. The position of the cupboard or shelf would be adjusted so that the smallest person could reach in and grasp an item. This might be done within a particular household if someone were putting up shelves or a hanging cupboard.

Many homes also have people in them who are much smaller than the average height — children! Homes have to be designed to accommodate them.

Q 10

a How would you arrange a kitchen so that a seven-year-old could reach things like cornflakes?
b How would you prevent a young child from burning herself very badly by pulling a pan off the cooker?
c Do you think that small children will learn good table manners if the table is much too high for them?

Particularly where very young children are concerned, we often take advantage of their lack of height to prevent them from damaging our belongings or themselves.

Q 11

Give three examples of this, explaining each time where the damage lies and how it is prevented.

10.6
PRODUCT DESIGN

You have looked at two fairly simple examples of how differences in human body size will affect design. There are many other examples. Human size and shape are not, of course, the only things which are related to ease of use, safety, and comfort. Equipment such as cookers has a number of aspects which are related to these factors.

Q 12

a Make list of the factors which you think are important for ease of use, safety, and comfort in the design of a cooker. (Remember that cookers are also used by the inexperienced and the elderly.)
b Check some cookers against your list to see how well or poorly they are suited to people.

Q 13

a Now consider the design of a bath. What features are important?
b What floor coverings are used in bathrooms, and what are their features?
c Suppose you want to hang washing over the bath. How would you design the bathroom to accommodate this? Are there any problems?

BACKGROUND READING

SITTING PRETTY

In the West when we want to sit down, we look for a chair. In the East people are much more comfortable sitting cross-legged on the floor. That position supports the spine naturally. In parts of Africa they prefer to squat on their hunkers. These examples show how unnecessary a chair is; yet if you are not brought up to sit on the ground you may find it very uncomfortable to sit like that for any length of time.

Figure 10.15
An eighteenth-century family at tea. The woman sits up very straight.

Five or six hundred years ago in Europe chairs were only used by kings, nobles, and important clergy such as bishops. Ordinary people sat on the floor or on benches or stools. There was only support for the back if you sat next to a wall. If your trade was a sedentary one (meaning one that you sat while you did it), you sat on a stool or a bench. Gradually from the time of Elizabeth I chairs became more popular among all types of people. If you look at paintings of people shown sitting in chairs, from that time and later, you will see that they are never shown leaning against the back of a chair. The back of the chair was there more for ornamental purposes than to support the back and it was considered rude or a sign of weakness to slump or sprawl on a chair. In Victorian times, even when new inventions in upholstery had helped to make chairs and sofas much more comfortable, young ladies would be told off very severely if they did not sit upright and away from the back.

Nowadays we have many different kinds of chair. This is partly because so many people spend their working days largely sitting down and the kind of chair varies according to their job. A typist's chair must be adjustable in height, and allow the typist to sit upright with clearance for the elbows. Executives working at desks need chairs from which they can lean forward easily to write. They also may like a big chair to let the world know how important they are. Chairs used for meetings are generally upright like dining chairs: you should sit upright to pay attention. Chairs and sofas chosen for airport lounges are generally softer, because they are meant for tired travellers.

We can often find a similar variety in an ordinary house. We have different chairs to sit on when we eat from those we loll on in the evening listening to music or watching television. We learn to sit upright in baby chairs and sometimes in older houses you will see nursing chairs which are special low chairs on which mothers sat to give the breast to babies. Members of the family prefer different kinds of chair or they may all argue over one favourite one.

The kind of chair you favour can say a lot about your personality. How you sit on the chair can tell the world even more about your fitness, your mood, and your state of mind.

CHAPTER 11

Accidents and why they happen

11.1
SAFE OR DANGEROUS?

How often have you heard someone say 'as safe as houses'? Such an expression suggests that we think of houses and homes as places where we are safe from danger.

Q 1

Look up the definition of 'safe' in a dictionary.

When the front door is locked and bolted, and you are enclosed in a warm, comfortable place, protected from the dangers of the hostile world outside, do you feel safe? Should people feel like this?

One way of finding out about the safety of any particular place is to look at the statistics on deaths, injuries, and accidents relating to that place. On this basis, how safe are homes?

Figure 11.1

Look at table 11.1. It shows the approximate number of accidental deaths and injuries associated with various places each year. Perhaps houses are not so safe after all!

Accidents	Deaths	Injuries
Home	6500	800 000
Road	6500	330 000
Work	800	330 000

Table 11.1

Q 2

a What other places do we think of as safe?

b What places do we consider are dangerous?

In each case, explain why.

11.2
BEHAVIOUR AND RISK

It is clear from table 11.1 that our idea of home as a refuge from danger is wide of the mark. It may be that in thinking about homes in this way, we may be partly responsible for the frightening numbers of deaths and injuries. In other words, if we treated our homes more cautiously, and behaved less casually towards the equipment in them, we would be more aware of the possible dangers, and there might be fewer accidents.

The way in which we behave is affected to some extent by how much risk we believe is present. We do not, for example, wander across the road with the same casualness as we do across a park; we do not pick up a razor-blade with the same lack of caution as we do when we pick up a book. We know that some things are more risky or dangerous than others. At least some domestic accidents may happen because people do not appreciate how dangerous homes can be.

Figure 11.2
Risky behaviour? The workmen know the dangers and behave accordingly. (In one picture you can see a workman climbing up the righthand side of the tower of St-Martin's-in-the-Fields, London, attached by a safety harness. The other picture shows workmen at the top.)

Q 3

What things around the home do you think of as dangerous? Put them into categories.

Figure 11.4a
Don't allow children to play with matches.

11.3
WHAT IS AN ACCIDENT?

There are four definitions we need to think about when we decide what an accident is.

1 Accidents are events which cause damage or injury.

2 Accidents are events which are not deliberate or intentional.

3 Accidents are events which are unexpected or unanticipated

4 Although accidents may appear to happen very suddenly and unpredictably, it is clear that they are often the end results of a series of events.

11.4
ACCIDENTS, INJURIES, AND PRODUCTS

One of the main difficulties in studying accidents is deciding how to classify them. Part of the difficulty is that in some cases the word for the type of accident is the same as for the injury (for instance, cut or burn) and in others (for instance, fall)

various different injuries can result. Obviously we should try to classify accidents by their 'cause'. However, it is often very difficult to decide what does cause accidents.

Take an example of an elderly man, in worn slippers, walking across a dimly-lit room. He treads on a pin, starts to fall, in trying to stay upright grabs at the tablecloth, which pulls the teapot over, scalding him with hot tea.

Q 4
What caused the accident?

It is clear that this, and most other accidents, are the result of some complicated relationship between the people involved, the place where the accident happens, and the objects or products involved.

Q 5
How does this relate to the ergonomics which you studied in Chapter 10?

It has become common practice to classify accident types in relation to the people, the location, and the product.

Q 6
Do some people have characteristics which make them more likely to be involved in accidents? Make a list of them. (Think about mental ones as well as physical ones.)

Q 7
List locations around the home and garden which are likely to be the place where accidents can occur. In each case, explain what sort of accident is likely, and why.

Q 8
List common products used in homes which you think are likely to be involved in accidents. In each case, explain why.

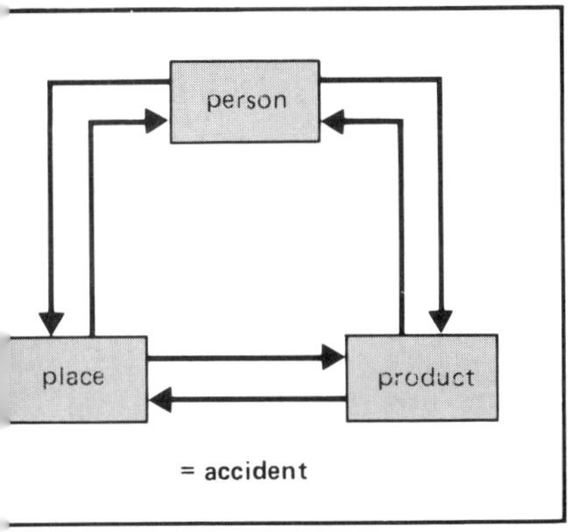

Figure 11.3
The interaction between the person, the place, and the product.

Figure 11.4b
Overhanging pan handles are very dangerous if there is a child in the house.

Figure 11.4c
This washing could easily fall and catch fire.

Table 11.2
Common types of home accident.

Accidents involving	Number	Per cent
Falls	24124	44.8
Cuts	10018	18.6
Being struck by an object	6699	12.4
Burns/scalds	3202	5.9
Poisoning	1385	2.6
Choking/suffocation	705	1.3
Electric current	64	0.1
Others/unknown	7698	14.3
Total	53959	100.0

Table 11.3
Types of injury resulting from home accidents.

Injury type	Number	Per cent
Cuts/lacerations	18743	32.9
Tenderness/swelling	7456	13.0
Fracture	6587	11.5
Bruise	5413	9.5
Sprain/strain	2649	4.6
Scald	1946	3.4
Burn	1873	3.2
Puncture wound	1426	2.5
Poisoning	1352	2.4
Others/unknown	8311	17.0
Total	57158	100.0

Table 11.4
Products and articles most commonly featured in home accidents.

Product category	Number of accidents	Product category	Number of accidents
Stairs/steps	6710	Tins/tin openers	1274
Doors (to rooms)	2659	Beds/bunks	1229
Chairs	1643	Tables	1130
Domestic knives	1517	Windows	949
Floors	1481	Hot water	926
Carpet	1387	Ladders/stepladders	919
Person (other than victim)	1308	Shoes/sandals	811

Table 11.5
Location of accidents within the home.

Location	Number	Per cent
Kitchen	8343	15.5
Living/dining room	7722	14.3
Inside stairs	5079	9.4
Bedroom	4882	9.0
Bathroom/toilet	1505	2.8
Hall/lobby	1173	2.2
Outside steps	947	1.8
Garden	5158	9.6
Yard/path	2590	4.8
Garage/shed	1042	1.9
Other/unknown	15518	28.7
Total	53959	100.0

Table 11.6
Age and sex of people involved in home accidents.

Age	Male	Female	Total
0 to 4	6835	4989	11862
5 to 9	3014	2157	5177
10 to 14	2173	1914	4093
15 to 44	8320	9305	17625
45 to 64	2852	4864	7716
65/over	1748	5694	7442
Total	24932	28944	53959

Q 9
Look at tables 11.2 and 11.3. What accidents are most common? What injuries are most common? Why do you think that the cause of so many accidents is unknown?

Q 10
Which product categories in table 11.4 are particularly unsafe? Why do you think this is?

Q 11
What particular accidents may occur in each of the locations in table 11.5?

Q 12
Look at table 11.6.
a Which groups of people are particularly at risk? Suggest reasons for these figures.
b Why do more women than men have accidents in the 'over 65' category?

11.5 ARE THERE MORE HOME ACCIDENTS THAN THERE USED TO BE?

It is only relatively recently that we have realized the size of the problem of accidents in the home. The number of deaths and injuries is horrifying, but should we be more worried now than we were a few years ago? There are at least four reasons why there has been increasing concern about accidents in the home.

First, homes today are full of the products of modern technology. These have often made our lives more comfortable and reduced drudgery, but at the same time they have brought new potential dangers.

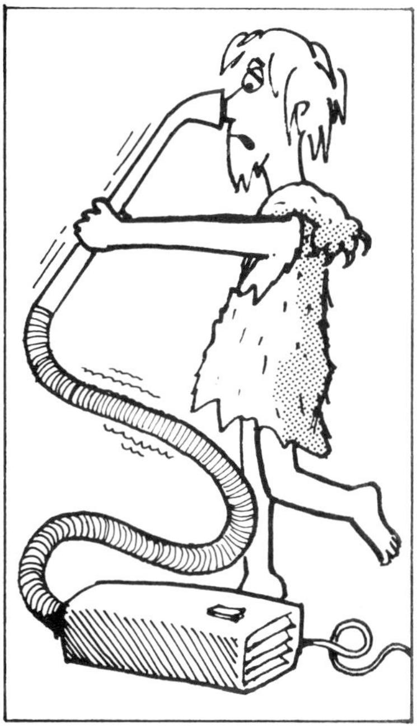

Figure 11.5
New technology brings new potential dangers.

Q 13
What products are now common in homes but were not so fifty years ago?

Q 14
What changes, if any, do these new products bring with them?

Second, with the rise in general consumer awareness, the idea that accidents 'just happen', and are largely due to carelessness, is less widespread. It is now commonly accepted that someone should be responsible for protecting people from dangerous products. You should be able to find warnings about dangers on the labels of many products.

Q 15
Who is responsible in this country for protecting consumers from dangerous products?

Third, during this century medical science has been able to control or reduce many other causes of death. Because of this, even if the number of home accidents had remained the same over the years, the number of deaths due to this cause would be proportionately greater.

Q 16
a What major diseases used to be common and are now much less so?
b What changes and developments have reduced the frequency and severity of these diseases?

Fourth, there is now a much better system of reporting home accidents. It may be that deaths and injuries resulting from accidents are now being recorded which would not have been previously included.

11.6
WHAT CAN WE DO ABOUT HOME ACCIDENTS?

Since we have suggested that accidents are a result of the relationship between people, places, and products, to prevent accidents we must alter this relationship. We can try to do this by altering each or all of the three factors.

Q 17
Is the above statement true? Is there any way that we can modify people physically?

We can attempt to alter the way they *think* so that they *behave* differently.

Q 18
What methods are used to attempt to influence people's behaviour?
How successful do you think they are?

We can try to improve the places where accidents tend to occur (see table 11.5).

Q 19
Suggest ways in which the places where most accidents occur could be modified to help avoid them.

We can change the products most likely to be involved with accidents (table 11.4) either at the personal level in the home or by legislation to compel manufacturers to improve their products.

Q 20
What other kinds of pressure could a community or an individual bring to bear on a manufacturer?

Find out what safety labels exist and where they can be found.

YOU WILL NEED:
Collection of labels from bottles, jars, etc.

1 Categorize the labels under the following headings: pills, garden products, household cleaners, household products such as aerosols, plastic bags etc, decorating materials, products for the car.

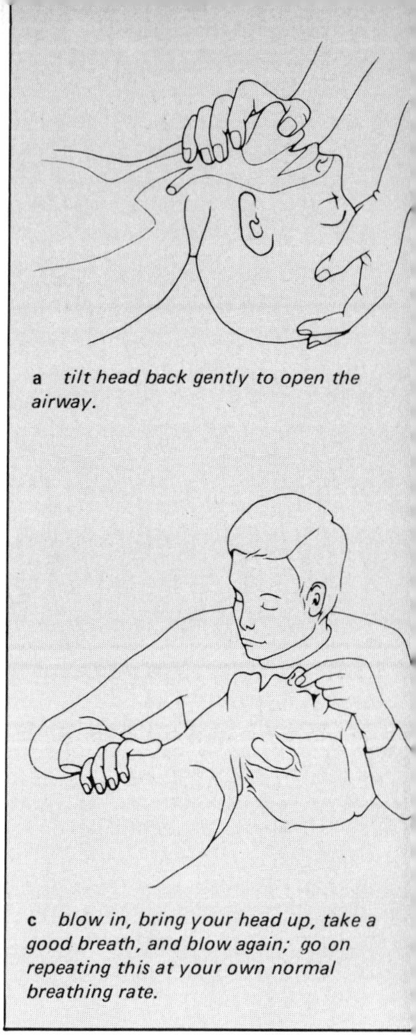

a *tilt head back gently to open the airway.*

c *blow in, bring your head up, take a good breath, and blow again; go on repeating this at your own normal breathing rate.*

Figure 11.7
Raise the limb to help to stop the bleeding.

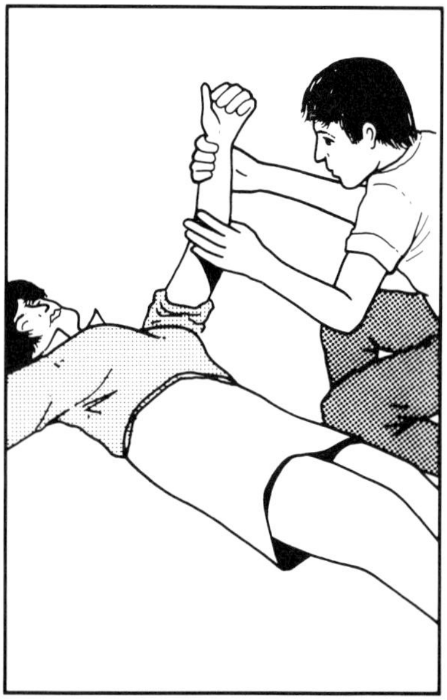

Figure 11.6
Mouth to mouth resuscitation.

b *hold nose closed while breathing into patient's mouth; feel chest rising with the other hand.*

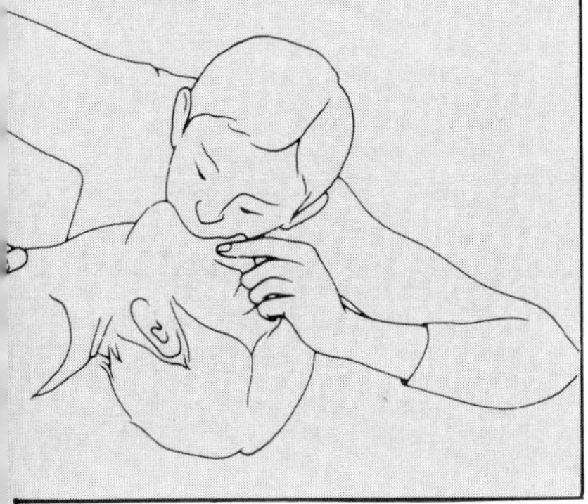

Figure 11.8
Bandage firmly: a handkerchief folded round a matchbox will form a pad and help to stop the bleeding.

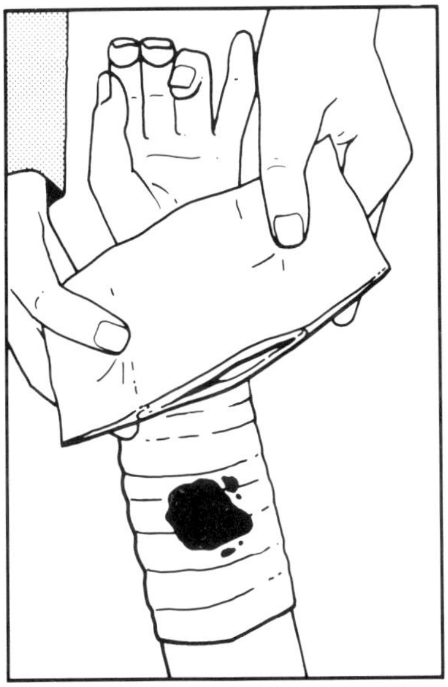

Figure 11.9
The recovery position.

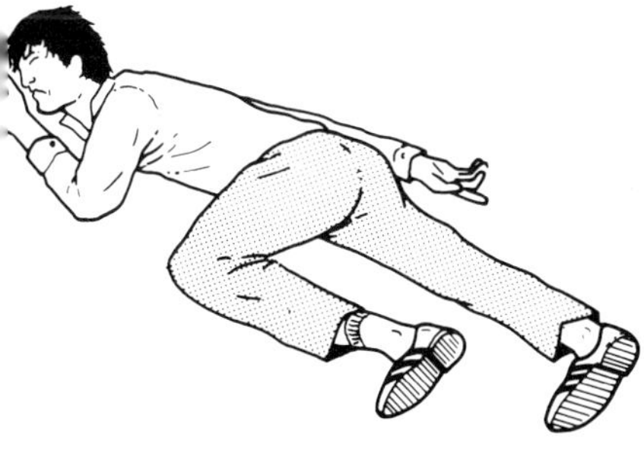

2 Extract the information which says that the product should be treated with care.

3 Decide whether the information is sufficient. Re-word the labels you think are inadequate.

Q 21
What more do you think could be done to avoid accidents from dangerous or poisonous substances in the home?

BACKGROUND READING

WHAT TO DO IF THERE'S AN ACCIDENT

Some home accidents can be very serious. Act quickly but don't panic. The framework of essential First Aid is based on four priorities. Is the casualty in any further danger? Is he or she breathing? Is she bleeding? Is she unconscious? When these matters have been attended to the casualty may still need medical help. For an ambulance dial 999. Speak clearly. Ask for an ambulance. Give your address and what you think is wrong.

Breathing: if someone is knocked unconscious, their tongue may fall back and choke them (see figure 11.6a). Tilt the head back and push the jaw forward so that it juts out beyond the nose. This opens the airway. You may well be rewarded by a life-giving gasp of air. If this does not work open the mouth and throat to see if there is an obvious obstruction. If there is, remove it. If there is still no breathing try *mouth to mouth resuscitation*. Figure 11.6 shows you how to do this. Continue until breathing is restored and/or until expert help arrives.

Bleeding: serious bleeding must be stopped quickly. Blood flows along veins and arteries which are like rubber tubes, so you can stop it by squeezing the end of the tube. The blood will also not run as fast if you make it go uphill, so raise the arm or leg (as long as it is not broken). Grasping the sides of a wound will squeeze the cut ends of the tube. As soon as you can, replace the pressure of your grasping fingers by the pressure of a pad and bandage, bandaging firmly. You may not have a First Aid kit — improvise (see figure 11.8). Do not give anything to drink and particularly do not give alcohol.

Unconsciousness: the cause does not matter very much. What does matter is the treatment. You have to keep the patient alive and breathing until the ambulance arrives. Keep the head tilted back and the jaw jutting forward. Give mouth to mouth resuscitation if breathing stops. Another danger is that they might drown in their own body fluids — mucus, saliva, blood, or vomit may run into the air passages. To get rid of these fluids we have to make the air passages run downhill to the mouth. Put them in the recovery position (see figure 11.9). Then check the airway again and keep the jaw jutting forward.

These hints are no substitute for a thorough knowledge of First Aid. St John Ambulance hold First Aid courses throughout the United Kingdom. Look in a telephone directory for details.

CHAPTER 12

'Home economics'

Figure 12.1
Good management, including the careful use of available funds, is essential in places like hospitals, airports, and railway stations.

12.1
WE EXPECT GOOD MANAGEMENT

We expect the bus company to run an efficient service that will be reasonably priced and provide buses at scheduled intervals; we expect our local council to run its services well — from road repairs to emptying dustbins; we expect hospitals to be competent at the vital work they do; and we expect local shops and stores to stock a wide range of goods that are available when we want them.

Q 1
What services do *you* expect to be well managed?

The same should be true of the way you organize your home. Of course, you do not want it to be so rigidly regulated that it is like being in the army all the time, but, on the other hand, if it is badly managed, all kinds of disadvantages can follow. If, for example, you do not plan ahead, you can get caught out by events catching up on you; or if you do not keep some records of your affairs, you will find them difficult to deal with. If you are careless in the way you spend your money, there may be too little left for essentials.

Many of the problems that arise in the home are the result of poor management of the money that is available.

Q 2
Think of a recent example where you did not manage your money as well as you might, and a problem occurred as a result.

Figure 12.2
Simplified model of a domestic water system.

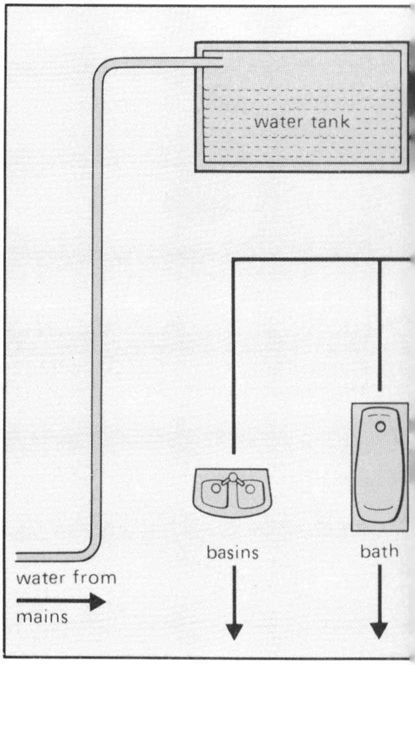

Figure 12.3
Poor money management.

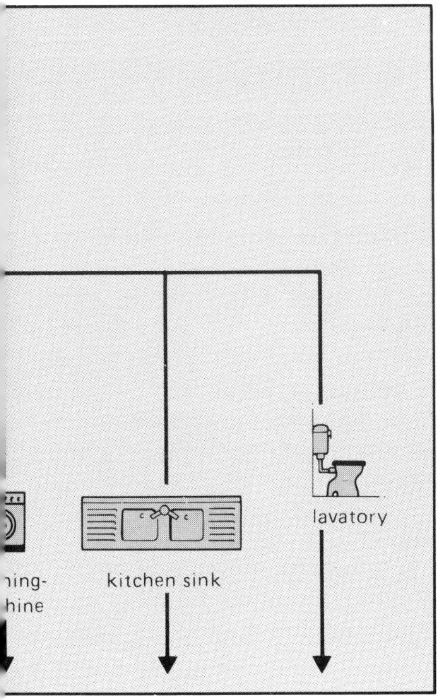

Q 3
How might you have organized yourself better, to have prevented this?

In Chapter 7, you studied the water system in your house. This system also helps us to learn about the use of money in the home. Water comes into the house from the mains, and is stored in a tank until it is needed. You may use it in all sorts of ways: through taps in washbasins and the bath, through a washing machine or dish-washer, and through lavatory cisterns, and so on. The used water goes out of the house, and the tank is topped-up again from the mains supply.

Money 'flows' in a similar way. It is brought into the home; it is stored temporarily until it is needed; it is used in a variety of ways; and, after it has gone, it is replaced. The problem is that, unlike the supply of water, money is not replaced immediately after it has been used. It is replaced a week or a month later, and, in the meantime, the store of money slowly goes down.

Q 4
What precautions would you take in your use of water around the house, if you knew that you had only a limited amount that you could use in any one week?

Q 5
Apply the answer you have given to question 4 to the situation shown in figure 12.3, by making a short list of 'rules' that you think would be helpful.

12.2
INCOME

Income is the 'flow' of money coming into the home. It may come from a number of sources. Here are the main ones.

Student grant
Supplementary benefit
Unemployment benefit

Wages from your job
Wages from the work of a relative who lives with you
Profit from your own business

Interest on money that is kept in a deposit account
Dividends on shares that you own
Sale of valuable possessions

Child benefit
Rent from someone who shares your home
An inheritance

Q 6
Why is 'pocket money' not included on this list?

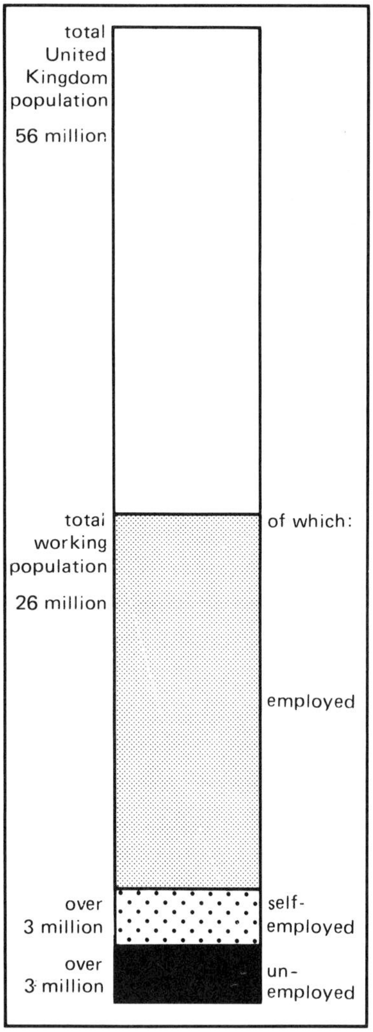

Figure 12.4

Figure 12.5

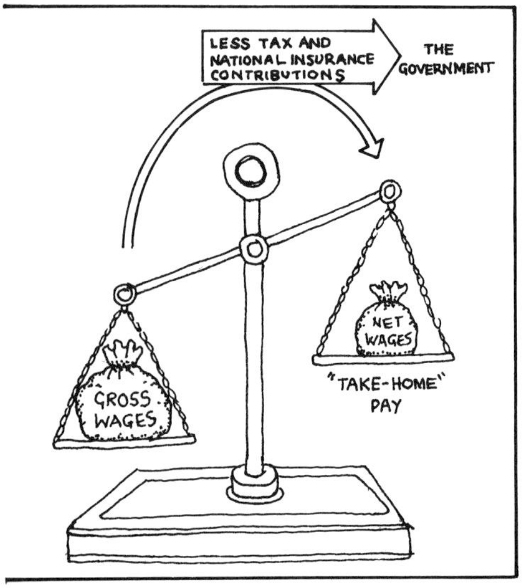

Q 7
What do we call the form of income that is paid to people who have retired?

Q 8
Write out the list of forms of income given on the previous page, and tick those which are likely to apply to you,
a in a year's time;
b in five years' time.

From figure 12.4, you can see that of the 'working' population, most people are 'employed'. This means that they work for someone else: for another person, or a company, an institution or organization, or for a local authority or the government itself. Most of the income coming into homes will, therefore, be in the form of wages, which are normally paid at the end of each week or each month. (When payments are made weekly, we tend to use the word 'wages'; for monthly payments, we tend to use the word 'salary'.)

Before making these payments, a British employer must first deduct any Personal Tax and the National Insurance Contribution from your pay. This is done under a system known as Pay-As-You-Earn (PAYE, for short). The amount deducted will depend on how much you earn; but, if you have just started work, you can roughly estimate that your total deductions will not be less than 10 per cent of your total wages, but not more than 25 per cent either. What you have left is your 'take-home' pay. Unless you have any other form of income, this will be the limit of your supply of money for that week or that month.

Q 9
Suppose you earn gross wages of £60 per week. What is *a* the most, and *b* the least that you are likely to 'take home' after deductions have been made?

Good management in your home will depend on your ability to live within your income, over that period of time.

TAX

Payments made to us by the British Government (such as a student grant, or supplementary or unemployment benefits) are not usually taxed at all, because those who receive them cannot afford to pay tax on their income.

Wages paid to us by an employer are 'taxed at source': that is, Personal Tax (as it is called) and the National Insurance Contribution are deducted from our pay before we receive it. We have left our 'take-home' pay.

Personal Tax and National Insurance Contribution are also paid by those who are self-employed. It is worked out according to the net profit of their business.

Other forms of income may be taxed 'at source' (such as the interest on a building society account or dividends paid on the shares we own), or may be left to us to 'declare' to the Tax Office, such as rent that we receive, or the profit made on the sale of certain valuable possessions.

In some cases, the amount of income may be too little for any tax to be payable; but the law requires that all our income is declared, and where the combined amount is very high, we may have to pay additional tax as well.

Figure 12.6
Mobile note cage used to guard bank notes during transit.

12.3
STORAGE

Water is so plentiful in Britain that — quite obviously — no-one is going to want to steal it from your tank at home. You can store it there safely. Money, on the other hand, is far more vulnerable: if you keep your income at home, you run the risk of it being stolen. Even more likely, perhaps, you run the risk of being easily tempted to spend it carelessly. However, despite the risks, some money will need to be kept in the house.

Q 10
Make a list of reasons why you sometimes need to have cash on you, or stored at home.

Figure 12.7

Any money that you do not need immediately should be kept in either a bank, a building society, or at the post office. All of these institutions offer a number of different accounts in which you can keep your money in complete safety.

Before deciding which type of account to open, call at your post office, and at local branches of banks and building societies. Ask for their information leaflets, judge how helpful you find them to be, and have a brief look around.

Table 12.1
Summary of main types of account.

Banks	Building societies	The post office
Current account Take your money out without giving notice Cheque book provided Usually no interest is paid Overdrafts are possible *Deposit account* Take your money out without giving notice Fair rate of interest paid on your money	*Share or deposit account* Take some of your money out without giving notice Interest paid on your money, with tax deducted first Helps when you want to obtain a mortgage Open Saturday mornings *High interest accounts* These vary from society to society: they usually pay good interest, but require notice before taking money out	*Ordinary account* Take up to £100 out without giving notice Interest paid on your money: £70 of interest tax free each year Open Saturday mornings Often long queues *Investment account* One month's notice needed before taking money out Good rate of interest paid on your money

Q 11

Arrange the questions below into the order in which they are the most important to *you*.

Q 12

Using the leaflets you have, your own observations, and by reference to table 12.1, very briefly answer *each* question for *each* type of account you are considering.

a Is the branch of the bank or building society or the post office open when I need it, or does it have a wall machine I can use when it is closed?

b How easy is it to take my money out when I need it?

c Do I want to keep my money there long enough for it to be worth while considering the interest it might earn?

d Is the interest already taxed, and does that matter to me?

e Must I open a bank account anyway? (Some employers pay wages directly into their employees' bank accounts, so you need a bank account before you can work for them.)

f What other services are being offered to me, and are these likely to be genuinely useful?

g Which sort of financial institution would I prefer to deal with?

From the information you obtain, it should begin to become clear which type of account is likely to suit your particular requirements best. If no single account offers you all the benefits you are looking for, it is quite usual to open a second account. For example, you might choose a bank current account to keep the money you know you are going to need in the near future, and to have the facility of a cheque book; but you might also choose a building society deposit account for your long-term savings, where your money earns you interest, until you need to take it out.

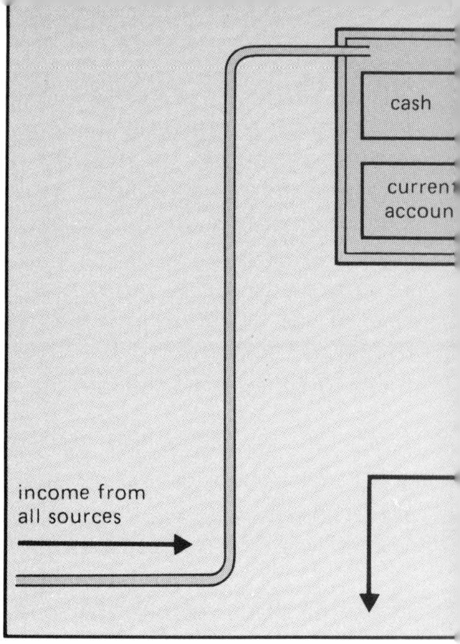

Figure 12.9
Some items we spend money on.

12.4 SPENDING

Figure 12.8 shows us the stage we have now reached. Before you move on, look again at your answers to questions 4 and 5.

There are only two ways of using your store of money:
1 you can spend it *this week*, or
2 you can save it this week, in order to spend it *later*.

Q 13

Make two lists of things that you spend your money on at present: write one list under the heading of 'spend this week', and the other under the heading, 'spend later'.

Q 14

Now repeat this exercise as if you were the person running your own home.

The money that you are likely to need to spend this week is probably best stored safely at home, while money that is to be

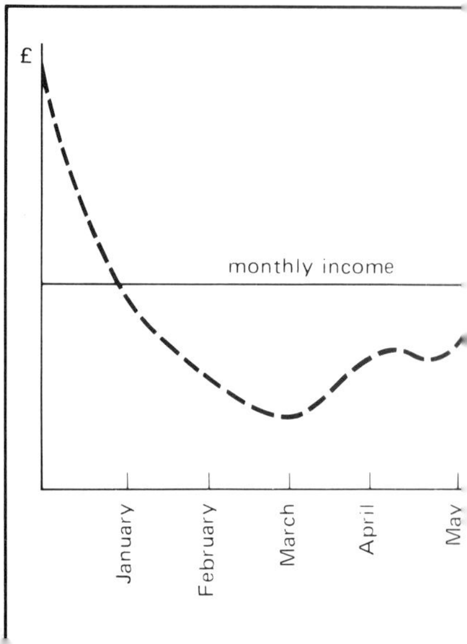

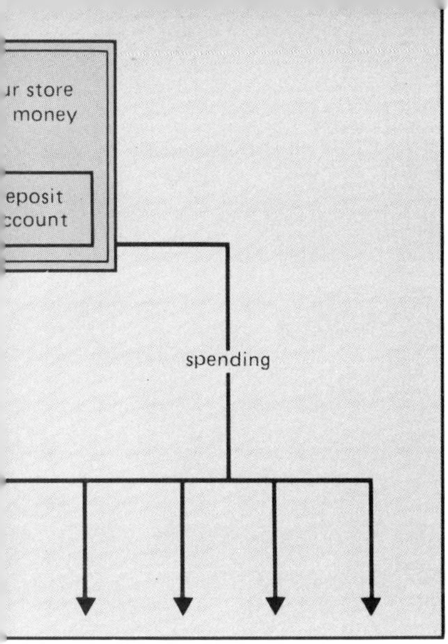

Figure 12.8
The flow of money through the home.

spent later should be put into one of the accounts shown in table 12.1. The account you choose will depend on how much later you will need to spend the money.

Q 15
Which account would you choose for
a money that you expect to spend in the next week or two, and
b money that you do not intend to spend for several months yet?

Some items on which you will have to spend money need to be paid for at monthly intervals, others quarterly (that is, every three months), others half-yearly, and some only need paying annually. Here is an example of each:

Weekly: the milk bill;
Monthly: rent;
Quarterly: electricity bills;
Half-yearly: water rates;
Annually: television licence.

(But even with these examples, there can be exceptions: the television licence can also be bought with television stamps, which you buy whenever you decide that you have the money to spare; rent may be payable weekly, and not monthly, and so on.)

Figure 12.10

Figure 12.11

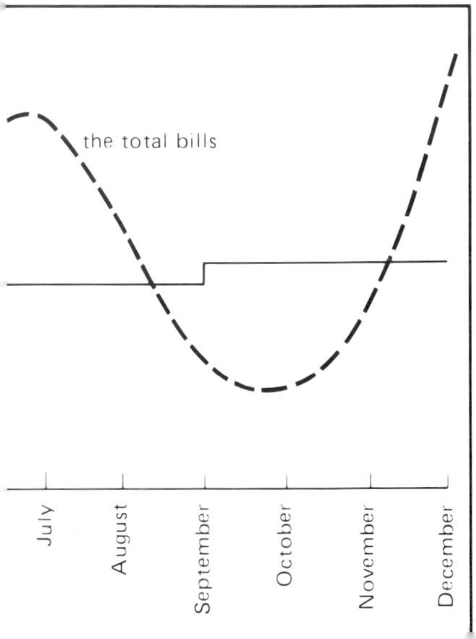

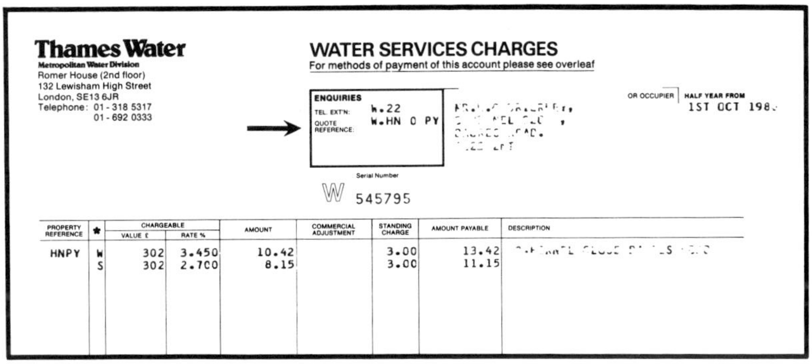

Thames Water
Metropolitan Water Division
Romer House (2nd floor)
132 Lewisham High Street
London, SE13 6JR
Telephone: 01-318 5317
01-692 0333

WATER SERVICES CHARGES
For methods of payment of this account please see overleaf

ENQUIRIES
TEL. EXT'N: W.22
QUOTE REFERENCE: W.HN O PY

OR OCCUPIER
HALF YEAR FROM
1ST OCT 198[illegible]

Serial Number
W 545795

PROPERTY REFERENCE	★	CHARGEABLE VALUE £	CHARGEABLE RATE %	AMOUNT	COMMERCIAL ADJUSTMENT	STANDING CHARGE	AMOUNT PAYABLE	DESCRIPTION
HNPY	W	302	3.450	10.42		3.00	13.42	[illegible]
	S	302	2.700	8.15		3.00	11.15	

Figure 12.12
A sample bill for Water Rates: payable half-yearly.

Q 16
Take the lists that you compiled for your answer to question 14. In order to see when you would normally pay for these items, write them out again, each under one of these headings:
weekly, monthly, quarterly, half-yearly, annually.

12.5 PROBLEMS

Having to pay for things at these different intervals can lead to a number of problems.

Q 17
Study figures 12.10 and 12.11, and then write down three problems that can result from having to pay bills in this way.

To solve problems like these, it is essential that
1 you know what to expect, and
2 you plan ahead accordingly.
Most good management relies on these two important rules.

Q 18
Give two important pieces of information that you think you would need to know in advance, if you were asked to plan:
a a wedding reception
b making the costumes for a play
c your household's spending.

In order to plan your household spending, you will need to know *what* bills you have to pay, *when* you have to pay them, and *how much* they are each likely to be. You should record this information on a table, like the one in table 12.2.

Month	Which bills?	Estimate (£)
January	gas telephone Paul's birthday	20 25 10
February	TV annual rental	114
March	electricity rates water rates	160 180 30
April	gas telephone	10 25
May	Jill's birthday	10
June	electricity insurance	120 60
July	gas telephone	10 25
August	holiday	150
September	electricity rates water rates	90 180 30
October	gas telephone TV licence	15 30 58
November	—	—
December	electricity Christmas presents	120 100
Total for whole year		1572

Table 12.2
Example of a household's annual estimate.

Q 19
Look at the gas and electricity bills in table 12.2.
a Why do the amounts of these bills vary throughout the year?
b What can you do to reduce these bills?

Q 20
Now look at the telephone bills.
a The estimate shows the same amount for the first three quarters of the year, which indicates that the telephone is likely to be used about

the same amount all the time. So, why has a slightly larger bill been estimated for the end of the year?

b What can you do to reduce your telephone bills?

Q 21

Now consider the average cost.

Suppose table 12.2 is the plan of your household spending over a year. Work out how much you would be paying

a on average each month (divide the annual total by 12)

b on average each week (divide the annual total by 52).

Q 22

Why do you need to work out the average cost, either per month or per week?

THE GOVERNMENT BUDGET

Each year, a 'budget' is prepared by the Chancellor of the Exchequer. It is his job to plan the government's spending so that it is kept within the limit of the government's income, from taxes and other sources.

Local councils and almost all businesses also draw up their own 'budget' each year. It is an excellent way to manage money properly, and one which we should follow in the home. We must plan our spending so that it stays within the limit of our income.

12.6
YOUR BUDGET

There are four stages in making out a household budget.

1 Be sure that you are clear how much income you are 'taking home' each week, or each month. Never budget on the basis of your gross wages.

2 Calculate the average amount (weekly or monthly) to put aside from your income, in order to pay the quarterly, half-yearly and annual bills. This money is probably best kept in a deposit account — although this will depend on how long it will stay there, before bills need to be paid from it. If you need help, either with making the calculation itself, or with running the account, you can always open a Budget Account, which can be operated for you by your bank. Call in at a local branch and ask for details.

3 Calculate the amount of your regular bills, whether these occur weekly or monthly. These would include all the family's food bills, travel to and from work, the rent or the mortgage payment, and so on. This money will also need to be put aside from your income, possibly in a current account (which would allow you to make payments by cheque), or, in small amounts, it could be kept in cash. But do not be tempted to spend it on anything else.

Figure 12.13
Three examples of government spending: a special school for deaf children, public works, and old people.

4 Only after all these amounts have been put aside, are you free to spend the remainder of your income on whatever you enjoy or want or need. Unfortunately, you will find that there is not likely to be much left over, especially if you also run a car. Moreover, you may want to save some of this money — either for something special in the future, or in case of an emergency.

Figure 12.15 shows the 'flow' of money through a home in the course of one week. Obviously, the intention will be to 'balance' the amount being spent with the amount of money coming in.

Q 23
How much is there left 'free' to spend or save if the budget in figure 12.15 is to be balanced?

We begin to realize that there is more to good money management than we might have first imagined, and, 'getting our sums wrong' can often be one of the causes of real distress at home.

Q 24
Who, other than a bank manager, could advise you about how much your various bills might be?

Q 25
Under the heading of 'careful spending', compile a list of recommendations that you think would help a person to keep spending under control, and not to waste money.

BACKGROUND READING

CREDIT
There are many meanings of the word 'credit', but it is referred to here as the arrangement by which it is possible to obtain goods or services, without paying their full cost at the time of receipt; or by which a sum of money is lent, and then is subsequently repaid, usually in instalments.

Some forms of credit are provided without charge: certain household bills, for example, can be spread over a period of time without incurring any extra cost, and many shops and mail order organizations provide free credit to customers buying their goods. Such arrangements can benefit the customer, who might otherwise not be able to afford the goods or service concerned, although there is the temptation for the customer to buy simply because credit is available: the temptation to 'have now, pay later'.

But most forms of credit incur an extra charge: 'interest'. This is a payment calculated as an annual percentage of the sum borrowed, and repayable in addition to the sum borrowed. Any organization or financial institution that provides such credit is obliged, by law, to make clear to the borrower the annual rate of interest that is being charged.

Sometimes, credit is required only for very short periods of time: for example, a householder, unable to pay all the bills in

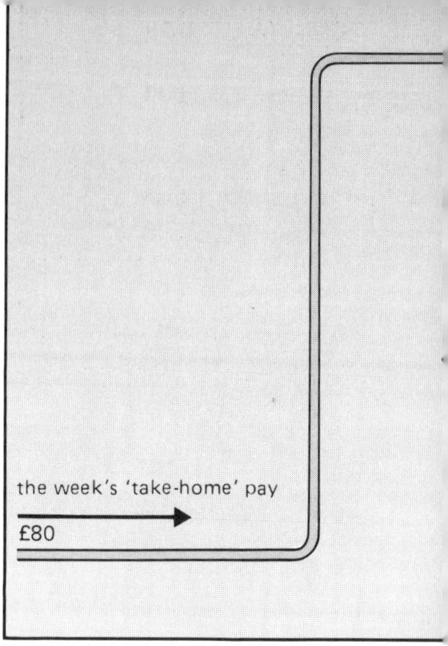

Figure 12.14
A mistake to avoid.

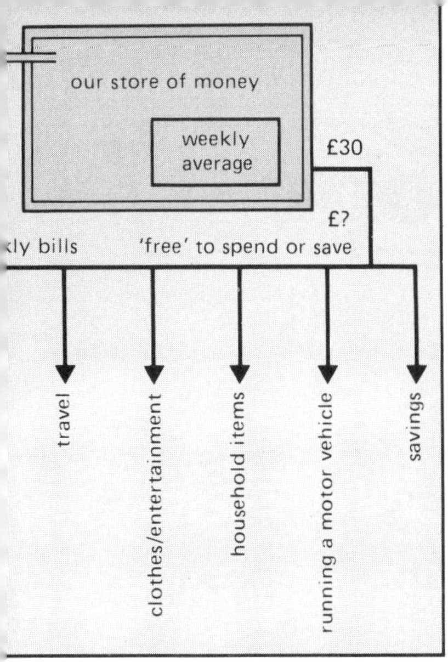

Figure 12.15
Example of a weekly budget.

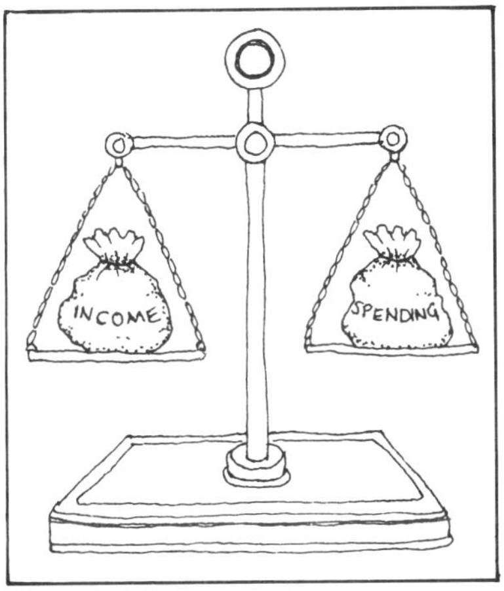

Figure 12.16
A balanced budget.

one particular month, may obtain a current account overdraft, or make use of a credit card, until the following month when the situation remedies itself. Such 'cash flow' problems are not uncommon, and banks are usually sympathetic when asked by customers for such short-term credit. From the householder's point of view, such an arrangement may be essential to good money management, and the cost of the interest may be a relatively small price to pay.

However, credit also takes the form of much larger amounts of money, repaid over much longer periods of time: a bank loan for home improvements may amount to several thousand pounds, and be repayable in monthly instalments over a five- or ten-year period. Mortgages, for the purpose of buying a house, can run into tens of thousands of pounds, and may take twenty or thirty years to repay. All such loans will depend on the borrower's level of income and on the extent to which the borrower can guarantee that level of income in the future. In these cases, the amount of interest that will be repaid in total is likely to be very substantial, and no-one should consider adding such a regular burden to their weekly or monthly budget, without carefully checking first that the repayments to be made can be afforded. While it is a benefit to obtain now some of the goods that it might take years to save up for, it has to be remembered that future spending will have to be reduced accordingly.

The most 'dangerous' forms of credit, however, are those that either come from a less than reputable source, or those that tempt people to spend without thinking first. Credit cards are often considered to 'burn a hole in one's pocket' and need careful use; understandably, the law prohibits their distribution to or use by anyone under the age of eighteen.

Today, with credit so much more readily available than it was in the past, people's attitudes to borrowing have become more relaxed; but that should not mean that we use credit casually or carelessly. Good money management must include also the proper use of the various credit facilities available.

Figure 12.17
Many shops offer credit to their customers.

Figure 12.18
Few people are ever likely to have a larger loan than a mortgage.

CHAPTER 13

Using technology

Figure 13.1
New technology.

13.1
WHY TECHNOLOGY?

Although we are still a long way from the perfect domestic robot, housework is very different from what it was even twenty years ago. In Chapter 8 you learned of the impact of electricity and gas as providers of energy to the home and how they have replaced human energy in many tasks. In this chapter you will consider the machines and other pieces of equipment which help to make running a home easier. The development of the microchip and its use in domestic products has already revolutionized some people's lives with things like video recorders, home computers, and cassette players. They are also used in modern cookers and washing-machines. However, it is unlikely that technology will ever completely replace human labour. It would cost a great deal of money to develop a robot that did not fall over the cat or choke the baby.

And there are other reasons for continuing with traditional methods. Homes are for people, not machines. Babies need to be picked up and cuddled, and most parents enjoy doing so. A baby-minding machine is only of limited use. Also, the efficiency of many old-fashioned methods does not encourage the development of automatic machines. There is a reluctance to try them by some workers in the home who prefer to use their hands rather than a machine.

Q 1

a Are there any tasks which you would rather do by hand, even though a machine is available? If so, list them and explain why.

b List those tasks which you would prefer to carry out using a machine, classified under the following headings: cooking, cleaning, other.

Figure 13.2
Comparing the efficiencies of different methods.

Figure 13.3

13.2 MACHINES WHICH HELP YOU TO CLEAN THINGS

As you know, dust, dirt, and rubbish is deposited on floors and furniture in the home. Clothes get dirty. Cookers, worktops, and other kitchen equipment become smeared with food and grease, as do crockery, cutlery, and saucepans. In addition to these physical causes of dirt, chemical changes take place on the surfaces of some substances: metals become rusty or tarnished.

Q 2
Why do you think it is necessary to clean things?
Are some cleaning jobs more important than others? Discuss which jobs you think need to be done frequently, and which can safely be left for days, weeks, or even months!

Many of these cleaning jobs can be done efficiently with the aid of machines. Machines for washing clothes have been developed over the past fifty years from the simple tubs with a powered agitator to the fully automatic machine which washes the clothes to a pre-set formula and then spins and tumble-dries them so that they can be used or worn immediately. Washing machines can be plumbed in to the main drainage system (see Chapter 7) which then frees the sink for other tasks. Smaller machines are portable and simply need an outlet from the sink and ordinary taps to supply hot or cold water.

Q 3
When do you think a tumble drier would be particularly useful? Are there any special problems which need to be taken into account before using one?

Modern technology has vastly increased the range of fibres from which textiles can be made, and has made the task of washing them more complex. The programmes available for washing textiles by machine are related to the fibres present and not to the garment which is to be washed. The kind of fibres must be known before selecting the washing programme which will clean

Figure 13.4
The Red Star washing-machine (c. 1905) and a modern machine.

Figure 13.5
Tumble-driers are useful but need to be used with care!

it satisfactorily without harming the fibres or causing the garment or article to shrink, stretch, crease, or otherwise spoil it. In order to help in identifying fibres and in choosing the appropriate programme a code of labels has been devised. These labels can be found on most garments and should be consulted before washing them. You may have learned about this in *Fibres and fabrics.*

Figure 13.6
An example of an HLCC care label.

Q 4
How would you deal with a pile of washing consisting of the following:
all-wool jersey
acrylic cardigan
50-50 wool and nylon socks, 3 pairs grey
80-20 wool and nylon socks, 2½ pairs green
pure cotton shirt, 1 white
poly-cotton shirts, 3 assorted, one with salad dressing spilt on it
newish blue cord jeans, very muddy and oily
selection of underwear including thermal vests and cotton knickers
2 towels
4 sheets and 2 pillowcases.
All to be ready for use tomorrow morning.

Do you know how different fabrics should be treated?

YOU WILL NEED:
Samples of different fabrics
Set of different fabric labels

Try to match each fabric sample with the correct label.

Great advances in cleaning agents have been made in the last few decades. Products of modern technology include detergents and enzymic detergents.

Q 5
What would your great-grandmother have done if she spilt black-currant juice all down her new summer dress?
What would you do now?

Figure 13.7

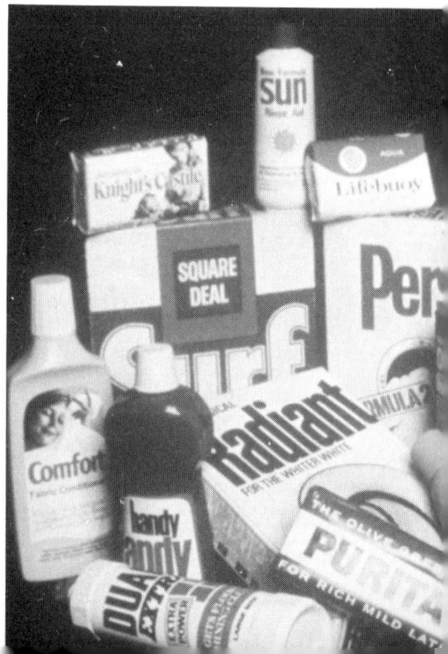

MACHINES FOR WASHING CHINA, GLASS, AND COOKING UTENSILS

Dish-washing machines are less commonly found in private homes than are clothes-washing machines. They can cope very easily with plates, cups, saucers, glasses, etc, but there are some problems with cutlery and cooking utensils and equipment.

Q 6
Why are dish-washers less common than clothes-washing machines?

Q 7
Why do dish-washers not clean saucepans and frying-pans effectively?

Q 8
Make a table which illustrates the advantage of using a dish-washing machine against the advantages of doing the task by hand.

Figure 13.8
Soaps and detergents old and new.

13.3
MACHINES FOR CLEANING THE HOUSE

The vacuum-cleaner is one of the oldest pieces of electric equipment used in house cleaning. It revolutionized the endless task of cleaning carpets and floors and removing grit and dust from surfaces and furnishings. Electrically powered floor-washing machines and polishers are now available too.

Q 9
Make a list of all the machines you know of which are available to help in the efficient cleaning of the home. Categorize them under the following headings:
floors and other surfaces, dishes, cooking utensils, clothing, bed-linen, soft furnishings, carpets, tiles, laminated plastic, glass.

Q 10
Which ones do you think are most useful? If you were setting up home with £300 to spend on such machines, which would you buy? Which would you save up for? Which would you consider unnecessary?

Figure 13.9
An advertisement for an early vacuum-cleaner.

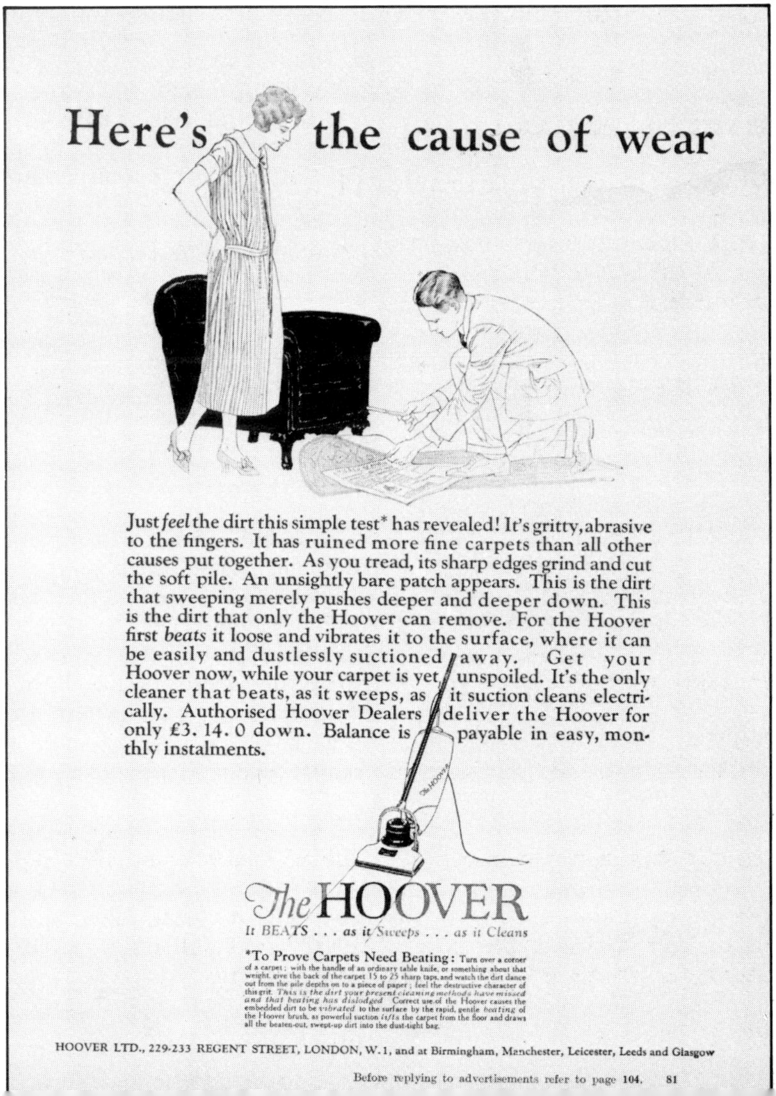

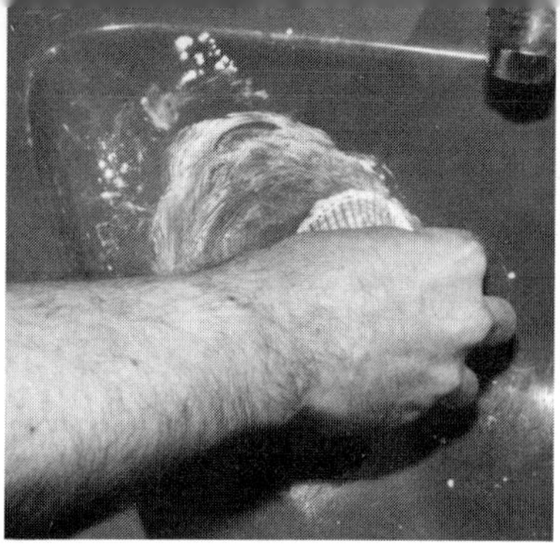

Figure 13.10
Using an abrasive cleaner.

Figure 13.11
The effect of different cleaners on a stainless steel sink unit drainer (magnified 500 times)
a *before cleaning*
b *cleaned with harsh powder scourer leading to damage*
c *cleaned with a cream cleaner right through to the shine.*

13.4
OLD-FASHIONED HARD WORK

Now consider the cleaning of cooking utensils and hard surfaces. Which abrasive cleaners are most suited to which items?

YOU WILL NEED:

Selection of surfaces:
set of patty tins
old non-stick frying-pan
old aluminium saucepan
old stainless steel saucepan
old enamel saucepan
white ceramic tile
piece of melamine (Formica, Arborite)
rigid plastic plate
piece of wood with adhesive PVC on it (Fablon, Contact)

Vacuum dust
Vegetable oil
Selection of abrasive cleaners, *e.g.* powder (Vim, Ajax), paste (Gumption), liquids and creams (Jif, Handy Andy)
Cleaning cloths (*e.g.* old vest or J-cloth)
Saucer or small basin for mixing
Flexible spatula (an old one)
Rubber gloves

1 Mix the vacuum dust and vegetable oil together with the spatula to make a stiff paste.

2 Spread the mixture thinly on each surface for an area of about 15 cm × 15 cm.

3 Leave it to harden for about 20 minutes.

4 When carrying out instructions *5* and *6*, time how long it takes you to clean each area;
count the number of rubs you give it;
remember how hard you have to rub.
Put your results in a table like the one in figure 13.12.

Surface	Cleaning agent	Number of wipes	Length of time	Amount of physical energy	Observation on results

Figure 13.12

5 Starting at one end of the strip, use the cream/liquid on an area of about 5 cm × 5 cm.

6 Use the paste and powder cleaners on the rest.

7 Examine each surface carefully, looking at it from a variety of angles. Write down your results in the table.

Q 11
Were these cleaning methods effective?
Do machines exist which would have done a better job?
When would you use a powder, paste, cream/liquid?
Which kind do you think is most useful for someone with a limited amount of time to spend on cleaning?

CLEANING METAL OBJECTS

Many homes contain tools, equipment, and ornaments which are made of metal. Silver and silver plate are sometimes used for cutlery and for other table ornaments; stainless steel is now more commonly used for these purposes.

Q 12
What are the advantages of using stainless steel tableware rather than silver plate? Are there any disadvantages?

Q 13
What other metals are used in the home? Why are metals used?

When metals tarnish, the surface of the metal reacts with the atmosphere or the things with which it comes into contact and a deposit of the metal oxide, sulphide, or carbonate is left on the surface. This chemical change spoils the surface, although it is not actually dirty.

Compare different ways of cleaning silver teaspoons.

YOU WILL NEED:

5 identical teaspoons (silver plate) with egg stains
4 aluminium bottle tops ('silver' milk-bottle tops washed and dried)
Silver polish in can; also impregnated wadding and liquid jewellery cleaner
Washing soda
Polishing rag and duster
Scales
Small boilable plastic bowl (500 ml)
Wooden tongs (small)
Clean tea-towel

Boiling water
Hot water and detergent in bowl for washing up

1 Try to wash off the stain on the spoons by ordinary washing up.

Q 14
Why do you think that this is not very successful?

2 Clean three of the spoons, using a different kind of silver polish for each one, and following the instructions on the can or bottle. Compare the results.

Q 15
Which method was easiest? cheapest? most successful?

3 Put the 4 clean bottle tops in the bottom of the plastic bowl.

4 Weigh out 25 g of washing soda and put it on top of the bottle tops.

5 Put one of the remaining stained spoons on top of the soda.

6 Pour 250 ml of boiling water over the spoon, soda, and bottle tops.

7 When the furious rising of bubbles has subsided, take out the spoon with the wooden tongs.

8 Leave the bowl and contents aside for at least an hour, overnight if possible.

9 Wash all the teaspoons in hot water and detergent. Don't mix them up! Dry them with the tea-towel.

10 Compare the teaspoon treated with soda with the others.

Q 16
Account for any differences in the teaspoons.

11 Re-examine the bowl containing the bottle tops and the washing soda.

Q 17
What has happened to the bottle tops?

Q 18
Do you think that it would be a good idea to use washing soda to clean very dirty, greasy, aluminium saucepans?
Give reasons for your answer.

13.5
MACHINES WHICH HELP YOU TO MAKE THINGS

Sewing and knitting machines are commonly used in the home. The sewing-machine has been around for a very long time and has made home dress-making and the making of soft furnishings and toys much easier and quicker.

Before food preparation machines were available, much time and energy was necessary in preparing meals. There were few 'prepared foods' available, which increased the scale of the task even more. Now many tasks can be carried out with a machine.

WHEN IS IT WORTH USING A MACHINE?

Many cooking tasks can be done either by hand or using a machine. Compare the preparation of some foods for yourself.

YOU WILL NEED:

Ingredients for making the following:

cole-slaw	meringue
batter	mayonnaise
pastry	bread-crumbs

1 Consult a cookery book for the recipes.

2 Prepare the foods, by hand and using a machine.

3 Make a table summarizing your conclusions.

4 Discuss your recommendations with the rest of your class.

Figure 13.14

Many other tasks in the home and garden can be done more easily with the aid of machines. Examples are: putting up shelves with the aid of a power or hand drill (could you manage without either?), and the different methods of cutting grass. You will be able to think of others.

The essential factor with all machines is the energy to drive them. Without the money to pay for external sources of energy, people have to rely on hand power.

Q 19
Where does the energy to drive a manual typewriter come from?

BACKGROUND READING

COMPUTERS IN THE HOME

Many homes now have microcomputers, but these are mainly used just for playing games — either of the arcade variety or more demanding ones such as chess. People often plan to use the computer to do their accounts, but soon tire of having to type all bills into the machine and go back to old-fashioned paper. If you have a lot of typing to do, adding a printer, a disc drive, and a good ready-made program allows you to turn the computer into a word processor. This can be a real labour saver.

We hear a lot about how, in the future, homes will be 'run by computer'. But what future developments are likely? One prediction is that a computer will be used to control all the electrical systems in the home: heating, lighting, security, and so on. This seems a bit unnecessary. A central-heating system can be controlled very well by a clock and a thermostat. It isn't hard to turn on a light. And perfectly good burglar alarms can be bought which don't need computer control. However, such systems could be useful for the disabled. Voice recognition systems are on sale for some computers: the disabled person could just say 'turn on the light' or 'open the front door' and the computer would do it.

The real benefits for most people are likely to come by linking their home computers into a larger network, so that they can communicate with large central data banks. You can already link any home computer into the telephone system with a device called a modem. You can also receive news and information on a specially-adapted television. British teletext systems are Ceefax, broadcast by the BBC, and Oracle from ITV. There is also British Telecom's Prestel, which comes in on the telephone line. If your home is on certain cable TV networks, you can use your computer to 'talk back' to the central computer of the teletext system. In this way you can deposit or withdraw money at your bank, order goods from shops, pay bills and so on. One bank offers a nationwide service, using Prestel and a special computer terminal supplied by the bank. More will follow.

And that isn't all. Already people with modems are calling up computer 'reference libraries' for facts they need — but these libraries are in America! Soon there will be local data banks you can consult. Doctors are now using computers to diagnose diseases, and to keep a record of the health of each patient. In a few years you should be able to consult your doctor's computer directly, without leaving home. A visit will only be necessary if your trouble turns out to be serious.

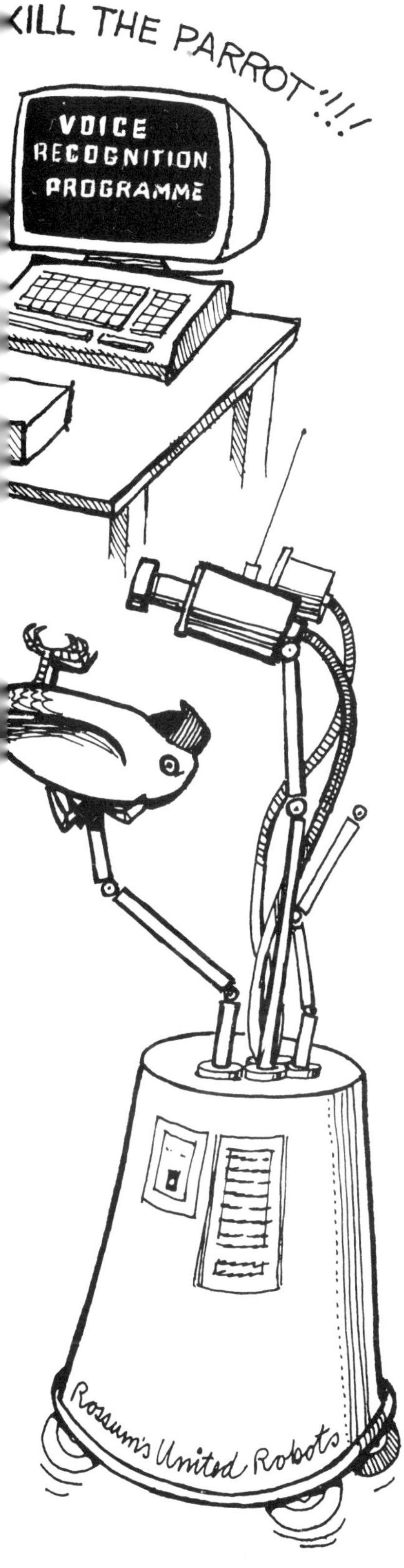

Figure 13.15

CHAPTER 14
Choosing and buying

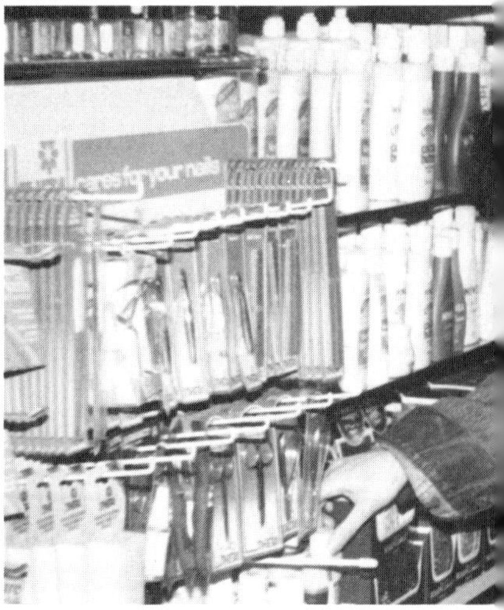

14.1
PEOPLE AS CONSUMERS

In the previous chapter you were asked to think about the home as a producing unit. In Chapter 4 you looked at teenagers as consumers and now in this chapter we are looking at people in general as consumers. By consumers we mean people who buy or obtain goods and services, that is, practically everyone.

So much is now available to buy in the shops in Britain that it is increasingly difficult to choose what to buy. In addition, many things are advertised in the press and on television. People may be confused about what is available and about how and why things are necessary or suitable, and so they often need help to enable them to choose wisely. This is particularly important when money is short. (You learned something about how to budget in Chapter 12.)

ADVISORY BODIES

Help is available from a variety of sources. Some people ask their neighbours and friends about their experiences with a particular product. Others will ask the shopkeeper or salesperson. Advertisements and the media may be sources of information. Magazines such as *Which?* can be consulted. *Which?* records the results of careful tests on a variety of brands of many goods and services including household equipment, cars, toys, and so on. It may be considered to give unbiased opinions since it is produced by the Consumers' Association. This is an independent body, and it does not carry any advertising or take money from manufacturers or suppliers.

Figure 14.2
Consulting 'Which?'

Q 1
Which sources do you think will give the most reliable advice? Why? What other sources can you think of? Which advice is easiest to come by?

Q 2
Look at the following list and suggest who or what you might consult before buying: motor-bike, bicycle, hair-drier, tape-recorder, pair of boots or shoes, suitcase or hold-all.

Figure 14.3

ADVERTISING

High on the list of people and things which influence us or help us to choose are the advertisers. Advertising goes on all around us, on billboards and signs, in newspapers and magazines, and on television. Advertising is very expensive — manufacturers are willing to spend hundreds of thousands of pounds for a single

Figure 14.1
Choosing between different brands.

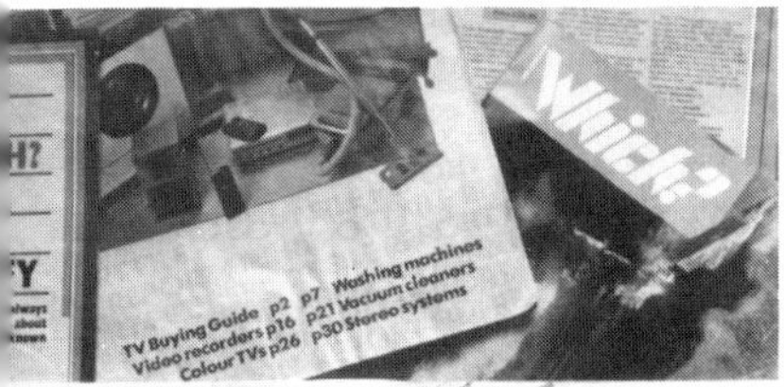

minute of peak-time television. Why? We may not think we are being influenced, but advertising is very powerful.

Are you influenced by advertisements?
Try this test. Make up a quiz based around current advertising slogans and ask a friend to fill in the missing word, like this:
. . . washes whiter.
Beans means . . . .

Sometimes the message we get is not as clear as it might be. Consider the following statements:
. . . lasts up to five times longer . . . .
. . . helps to remove stains . . . .
. . . you can't buy a better lipstick . . . .

Some advertisements may flatter you into buying — 'a perfume for the world's most beautiful woman!'

Assess the value of some advertisements for yourself.

YOU WILL NEED:
Pile of advertisements

1 Look at the selection of advertisements and decide whether or not they appeal to you or would influence your choice.

Q 3
What appeals to you about the ones that you think would influence you?

2 Try to categorize the advertisements, arranging them in separate piles, as follows:

Which attract children?
Which are aimed at teenagers?
Which are aimed at young families?
Which are aimed at old people?

Q 4
a Which of these groups do you think are the most vulnerable?
b Do you think that more should be done to protect them from advertisements?

Q 5
Which advertisement gives the most information? Is there anything else you would like to know about the product?

Q 6
How could you check the claims made for the product?

WHERE AND HOW DO YOU BUY?
When you have decided to buy something, the next thing to consider is where to buy it. There are quite a few alternatives — a department store, corner shop, mail order catalogue, or perhaps an auction.

Here are some factors to take into account when deciding where to go.

1 How much are you prepared to pay?

2 How much time do you have available for comparing prices or for travelling to a shop where you think it will be cheaper?

3 Is the shop easy to get to — is it near you, on a bus route, or is car parking easy?

Prices can differ even for the same article. Are there advantages in always buying from the same shop? You may find that it is worth going to a shop where you get personal service. Is there a large range available? Is the shop willing to change the goods you have bought? A large cut-price store may be much less helpful when you are making your choice or if your purchase turns out to be unsatisfactory. It may also not have a good atmosphere or room to move without being pressured to buy.

Superstores are normally thought to be cheaper than corner shops. You could compare prices of selected items for yourself. However, corner shops are very convenient when you are in a hurry and for people who cannot easily travel to larger stores.

You could find out about bulk purchases. How much money do you save? How easy is it to take home your purchases and to store them? 'Cash and carry' stores usually save money but there may be restrictions on who can shop there.

Shopping by post: what are the advantages and disadvantages of this? Look critically at catalogues and advertisements and compare prices with local shops.

Is the place of origin and/or where the article was made important to you? Do you approve of the slogan 'Buy British'?

Second-hand furniture and other items can sometimes be bought cheaply at an auction. Have you ever been to an auction? Try to find out how they work.

Figure 14.4
Two auctions — at Christie's and in a church hall in Newport, South Wales.

Figure 14.5
Buying from a jumble sale.

Wherever you decide to shop it is wise to have a clear idea of what you want to buy and, if necessary, make a list. A shopping list helps you to plan and control your spending. (Chapter 12 explained how important this is in household budgeting.) Buying on an impulse is rarely satisfactory.

Q 7
Select one item, perhaps a garment or a special food item, and list the possible places to buy it. Check with other people in your class and make a composite list of all the possible sources.

PACKAGING AND LABELLING

Packaging ranges from a simple plastic or paper bag to a fancy elaborate package which may even be difficult to remove.

The main functions of packaging materials are:
to protect the contents;
to advertise the contents;
to explain how they should be used;
to describe what they contain;
to make the product look attractive.

Labelling of food is now covered by law. As you may have learned in *Food science* and *Nutrition*, food labels have to state what the product contains. They sometimes also give nutritional information.

Q 8
Collect a variety of labels from both food and other items. How much information do they give you?
Compare how informative they are, making notes under the following headings:
health, safety, instructions for use, ingredients or materials it is made of, size and weight, price.

Figure 14.6
Buying from a market stall.

Figure 14.7
Packaging can be difficult to open!

14.2
WHAT IS AVAILABLE?

You will have noticed that several different appliances are capable of performing the same tasks. You may find yourself comparing two appliances and trying to decide which will make the best buy.

The simplest way to make a sound 'purchase decision' is to compare the two appliances with respect to several criteria (qualities), and to decide which criteria are the most important for what you want it to do.

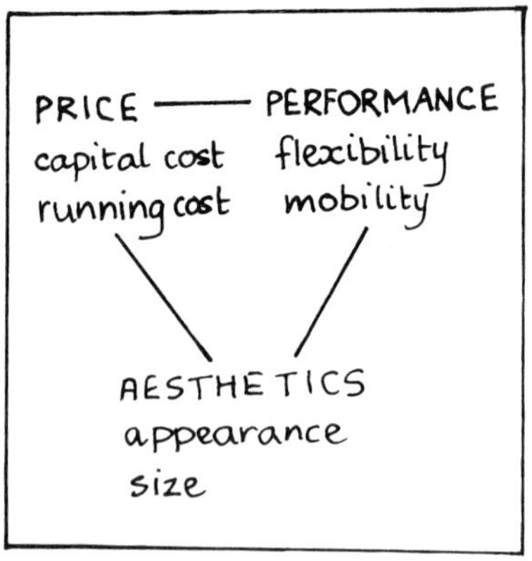

These criteria can be grouped under three main headings: price, performance, and aesthetics.

The three main criteria are inter-related; different people may consider one criterion to be more important. For instance, a student living on a budget is likely to place great importance on *price* and less on *aesthetics*, but will expect an appliance to *perform* well. You may have learned about these criteria in *Fibres and fabrics.*

If we apply these criteria to the purchase of a cooker then the following could be considered:

1 *Price:* its 'capital cost': what does it cost to buy?
2 *Fuel consumption:* how much fuel does it use; what are the running costs?
3 *Flexibility:* how many different cooking tasks will it perform?
4 *Performance:* how well does it perform these cooking tasks?
5 *Size:* is it large or small; does it fit the available space?
6 *Mobility:* is it portable; does it need to be portable?
7 *Appearance:* how attractive is it to look at?

Figure 14.8
How not to equip a kitchen — the fridge is jammed up against a radiator, and the doors of the washing-machine and tumble-drier open against each other.

The features which people might want on a cooker can vary considerably. For instance, automatic timers are useful if you want cooking to start before you get home; oven lights enable you to see what is going on in the oven; spits enable you to grill a wide variety of foods, such as kebabs; wheels or rollers make it easier to move the cooker out for cleaning.

Q 9
Think of three different types of people (such as someone living in a bedsit or an old person). For each one, list the cooker features you think they would want.

14.3
EQUIPPING A KITCHEN

The decisions that have to be made in order to equip a kitchen are probably amongst the most important because the equipment and furnishings are very expensive and will last a long time. It is therefore important to apply the criteria we have established in the last section to make sure that we make the right decisions.

You may have studied kitchen design in *The Basic Course.* Alternative layouts include galley, U-shaped, L-shaped, and a

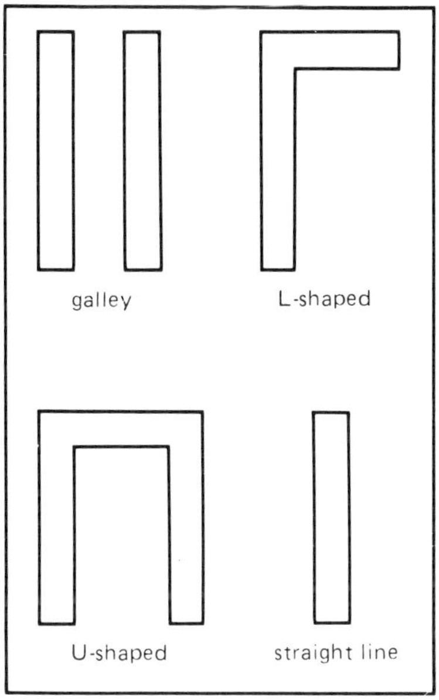

Figure 14.9
Kitchen layouts.

straight line (see figure 14.9 and worksheet M16a and b). Convenience, safety, and hygiene are all factors to be taken into account. The design of the kitchen is as important as choosing the right equipment. It is the most used room in the home and it needs to be attractive and pleasant to live in as well as efficient.

Q 10
List the equipment you think essential in any kitchen. Divide your list into:
what is likely to have been provided and is fixed into the room, and
the rest which will need to be bought.

A fixture such as a sink may very well control the position of the rest of the equipment you select. In this case, size may be an important criterion.

Q 11
a Look at your list and, using the groupings given in the previous section, decide the order of priority of the criteria for each of the items you need to buy.
b It is unlikely that you will be able to afford everything on your list from the beginning, but you now should be able to decide which are the most important. Try working within a budget of £1000: find out what you could buy locally for that amount. At the same time you could also discover what a further outlay of £1000 would buy.

Q 12
Now decide what you would need in a kitchen of your own.

14.4
THE LAW AND CONSUMERS

When you buy goods or services you enter into a contract with the person who supplies the goods or the services. This applies even to 5 lbs of potatoes bought from a market stall.

Figure 14.10
Shopping for kitchen equipment.

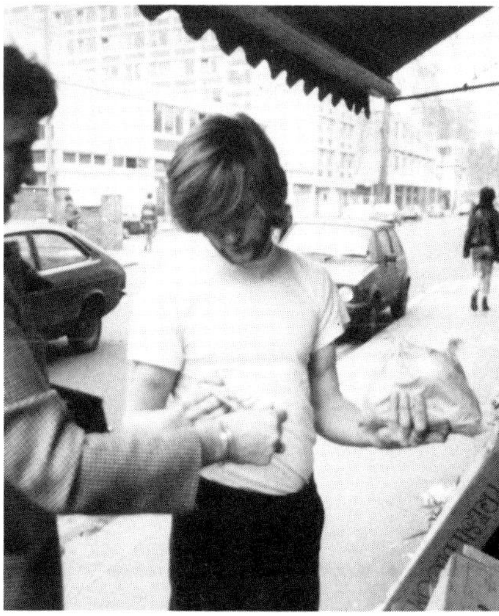

Figure 14.11
Making a contract.

In return for being paid for the goods, the shopkeeper promises that what he sells you will be as described, fit for its purpose, and of merchantable, or reasonable, quality. If any of these promises are broken you will be entitled to your money back. But not if a fault was pointed out to you before you bought the item, or if you got it as a present, or if you bought it from someone who was not in business.

Figure 14.12
Where to go for advice.

If you have bought something with which you are dissatisfied, what should you do?

First of all go back to the shop where you bought it, or write to the suppliers (not the manufacturers). Your contract is with the seller. If the goods are defective you are entitled to your money back. You need not accept a credit note. These are your rights under the *Sale of Goods Act*, and you can enforce them by taking the trader to court if he absolutely refuses to help you. If your claim is for less than £500 you can do this yourself without a solicitor, using the small claims procedure. You can get help and advice on this from your local Citizens' Advice Bureau or Trading Standards Department.

Sometimes, for instance if you are sold something which is short-weight or is mis-described, the shop may have committed a criminal offence. Someone who describes a plastic belt as 'leather' is breaking the *Trade Descriptions Act.* Your local Trading Standards Officer will want to know about this. He can investigate and may, in the end, prosecute the trader.

Figure 14.13

Q 13
Who else helps the consumer? Try to find out how the following organizations function.
1 The Office of Fair Trading
2 Citizens' Advice Bureau
3 The Department of Health and Social Security
4 The Design Council
5 Local Trading Standards Offices
6 The National Housewives' Register
7 National Consumer Council
8 British Standards Institution.

GUARANTEES

Have you ever received a guarantee for anything? Why do you think you were given a guarantee?

Q 14
a Read the guarantee provided by your teacher and decide whether you think they are useful and fair. (Look at guarantees for services as well as goods.)
b Read the terms and conditions of a service, for example, a dry cleaner or a holiday firm. Look at the small print and find out whether the guarantee covers all the problems which could arise.

BACKGROUND READING

SUPER-MARKETING

Several years ago, a study was carried out into supermarket shopping habits. Having positioned himself outside the local supermarket with clipboard and pencil, the researcher asked shoppers as they were going into the shop what they were intending to buy. On their way out, he stopped the same people and inspected the contents of their shopping baskets.

Despite the fact that these people had gone through their shopping lists with the researcher beforehand, nearly half the goods in their shopping baskets were things they had not intended to buy. Why did they buy the extra items? Some things were bought as 'treats', some had taken advantage of special offers, some had their memories triggered when they saw something, and some, when asked, couldn't think why they had picked up the extra item.

Inspection of the average supermarket layout would reveal that things did not get into their respective positions by accident. Have you ever wondered why supermarkets don't have one section containing basic household items like bread, sugar, butter, tea, and soap powder? Basic items like these are spread all over the store so that you have to pass up and down all the aisles in order to do your weekly shop. The more goods you pass, the more you're tempted to buy, and so the more they sell.

A great deal of thought is put into the positioning of high profit items like fancy biscuits, confectionery, and prepared meals. These items are likely to be placed at eye-level, in the middle of a display rack. In a freezer display, the 'hot spot' (in terms of selling, that is), is in the middle of the freezer. Here you might find stuffed and basted turkeys, or frozen prepared meals — products on which the shop stands to make a healthy profit. Basic frozen foods may be positioned at the ends of the compartment. Displays of sweets and chocolates are often placed at a child's eye level, by the till, so that mothers queuing with young children at the checkout may be pressured to buy, and people cannot eat the sweets as they go round the store and so avoid paying for them.

The store is not just being thoughtful by putting salad creams (a high profit item) next to salad ingredients, stuffing mixes next to chickens. In America when they placed vitamin pills next to a display of footballs the sales of vitamin pills rocketed! And the bigger the trolley the more you can buy.

Some supermarkets even use the extractor fans to pump the smell of freshly baked bread into the store, and at the entrance they display fresh fruit and vegetables to encourage shoppers to think that they sell fresh healthy foods.

So next time you're in a supermarket, try the test for yourself. Make a list and see how many times you are tempted to pick up something extra. Look at the labels, check the prices and ask yourself whether you are still tempted to buy.

CHAPTER 15

What is design?

15.1
WHAT DO DESIGNERS DO?

A design is a plan and record of the way in which a task can be carried out. Designers aim to offer solutions to the problems likely to be encountered in carrying out the task and to satisfy the needs of the individuals concerned. The use of appropriate materials and tools and the selection of colours, shapes, and textures will contribute to providing attractive and satisfying environments.

When carrying out a task, a designer will usually follow a set pattern of working. This is the 'design process'.

First stage. This is the brief or the identification of a need, a problem, or a market opportunity. This will require the collection of data and considerations of technological and economic constraints, and will involve experiments with materials and equipment.

Figure 15.1
Good design.

Figure 15.2
Architect at work.

Figure 15.3
'Cloud chair' designed by Nichola Spence from the Bosworth College, Leicester, for which she won a Design Council prize in 1984.

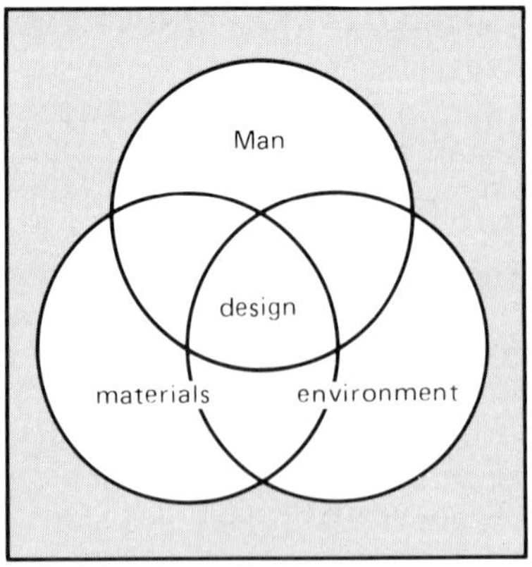

Figure 15.4
Nappy changer for use in public places, designed by Julian Webster from the City of Leicester School, for which he also won a Design Council prize in 1984.

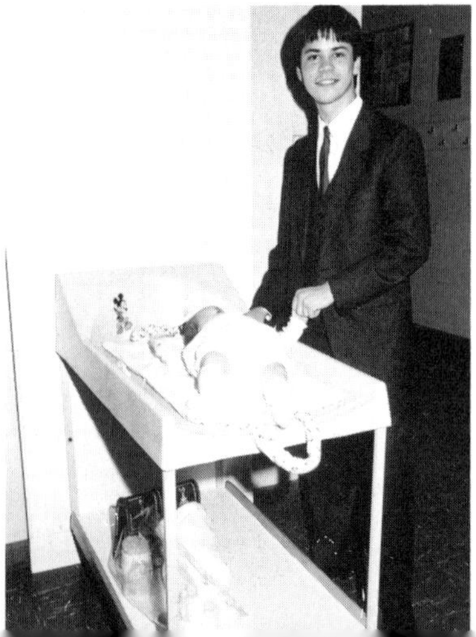

Figure 15.5
Two pictures from the Design Council's 'cautionary' section: a double bed and a three-piece suite.

Figure 15.6
A carefully designed cutlery rack.

Q 1
Make a list of the places where you might find information to help you with a design problem.

Q 2
Make a diagrammatic grid or flow diagram to show the ways that you might record this information.

Second stage. The development of ideas will involve possible solutions, rejected ideas leading to selected ideas, prototypes, and the preparation of instructions for production and programmes of work.

Q 3
Make a list of the points to consider when choosing materials. (See Chapter 14 and *Fibres and fabrics,* Chapter 1.)

Third stage. The marketing, use, testing, and evaluation of the product will result in an assessment of its effectiveness. You can now see to what extent the original brief has been fulfilled.

Note. At each stage, you should evaluate your progress and make modifications to the product before moving on to the next stage.

Q 4
What problems could occur before the final version is made?

Q 5
Suggest ways in which you could find out how successful your final version was.

Q 6
How could you advertise your final product?

15.2
ASPECTS OF DESIGN

Almost automatically a designer will consider colour, shape, and texture in relation to the materials to be used and the environment. It is the right combination of these values which should bring satisfaction and visual pleasure.

COLOUR IN THE HOME

The choice of colour in the home depends mostly on the personal likes and dislikes of the people concerned. They may be influenced by the aspect, the setting, and the uses to which the room is put.

Q 7
What is your favourite colour? Can you explain why?

Colours have different effects depending on what other colours they are with. Make a colour wheel and experiment with this for yourself.

YOU WILL NEED:

Card
Compass
Coloured crayons or paints

Q 8
Which are soothing colours?
Which are warm colours?
Which are cold colours?
Which are soft colours?
Which are hard colours?
Make a colour grid to illustrate your answers.

Q 9
Give examples of contrasting colours.
Give examples of harmonious colours.

Q 10
Describe the effects that the colours you have chosen could have on people's moods.

Q 11
Think about the colours of foods. Why don't we like blue piped potatoes or green bread and yet love red soup?

Q 12
Make a table like the one in figure 15.9 and fill in the appropriate foods under each heading. Do you notice any patterns?

Figure 15.7
Curtains and wallpaper in the same pattern.

Figure 15.8
William Morris pattern.

Red	Blue	Green	Yellow
Tomato		Cabbage	Lemon

Figure 15.9

SHAPE

The Victorians had a lot of different shapes and patterns in their homes. Today's furniture and furnishings are much plainer.

Q 13
Why are things shaped in a particular way? Draw two examples of things with corners, and two examples of circular things. In each case, explain why they are like this.

Q 14
Draw what you believe to be the four most used basic geometric shapes. Give examples of how these are used in the home.

Q 15
Round houses are not popular in Britain. Why?

Q 16
a Make a ground floor plan of your own home.
b Discuss the shape of the rooms with the rest of your class and make recommendations for
a a living room
b a kitchen
c the hall
d a teenager's bedroom.

PATTERN

We use pattern to provide interest and contrast. It may be used in an area in the room between plain areas and focal points. A room that has too much pattern may be overstimulating; a

Figure 15.10
A 'half-drop' pattern. This brocade was made in the sixteenth century.

Figure 15.11
Textile design from the 1970s.

Figure 15.12
Textile design from the 1930s.

room that is too plain may be uninteresting. Repeat patterns are useful because they slow down the vision and provide interest, without complexity.

Q 17
Where are patterns found in most rooms?

Q 18
What patterns are suitable for curtains?

Design some simple repeat patterns that could be used for curtains.

YOU WILL NEED:

2 pieces of cartridge paper
Coloured pencils or paints

Figure 15.13
Beware of too many patterns!

1 Divide the first piece of paper into 8 squares by folding it, and experiment with your ideas.

2 Select one idea, and follow it through on the second piece.

Patterns must relate to the material which is being used — curtains, carpets, wallpaper. Room size also determines the types of shapes and patterns which will give a pleasing appearance. Strong patterns make the room seem smaller and are not very restful. Small patterns can be used in small rooms to create spaciousness.

When choosing patterns for a room, you could use a bold pattern and other smaller patterns. Different patterns in a room can be linked by colour co-ordination.

Like colours, patterns and shapes must be in harmony with the use of the room.

Q 19
Design colour co-ordinated patterns which could be used on fabric for curtains, wallpaper, and quilt covers for your own room.

TEXTURE
This is very closely related to the medium which has been used for the manufacture of the article. They can be classified as warm or cold.

Q 20
Make a list of the words which describe *texture,* and then find an example from around the home for each one.

Q 21
Make a collection of different textures, *e.g.* using fabrics, fabric sculpture, knitted sculptures. Describe them and their function.

Figure 15.14
Careful thought is needed about the lighting in a room like this.

Figure 15.16
Example of an economically furnished living-room.

15.3
LIGHTING IN THE HOME

The function of the room in the house usually determines the type of lighting used. Daylight is greatly valued today, and more and more people are having patio doors which provide extra light and create a more spacious feeling to the room.

Artificial lights can be used to give a clear bright light or to give atmosphere to a room. Different effects can be created by altering the size, colour, and shapes of the artificial lights or their shades. There are various types of artificial lights available.

Q 22

Look at figure 15.17. Describe which types of lighting you would use in each of the rooms listed in figure 15.15. (Copy the table and fill it in.) Discuss your choices with the rest of the people in your class.

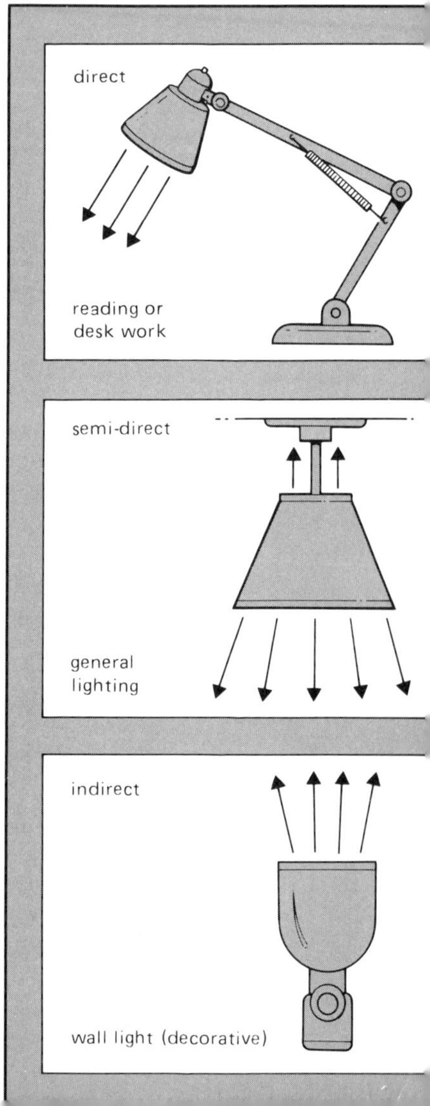

15.4
FURNITURE AND FURNISHINGS

The age and style of the house usually determines the type of furniture which will fit into the rooms and provide an attractive

Figure 15.15

1 Kitchen	
2 Dining-room	
3 Sitting-room	
4 Hall	
5 Stairs	
6 Bathroom	
7 Parents' bedroom	
8 5-year-old's bedroom	
9 Front door	
10 Study	

Figure 15.17
There are many different types of artificial light available.

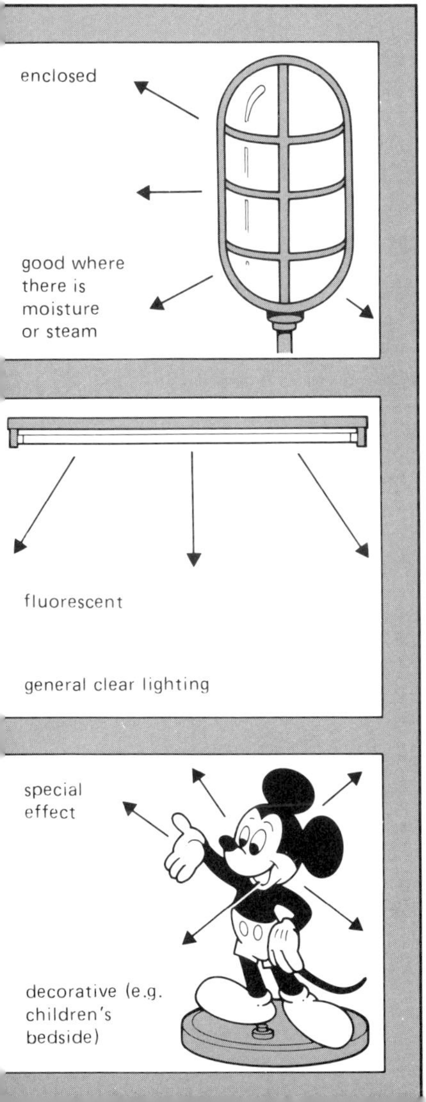

Figure 15.18
Example of an economically furnished kitchen.

environment. It is simpler to keep the same style of furniture and furnishings throughout the house. The exception is, perhaps, the kitchen; many old houses have very modern kitchens.

Q 23
Look through the property section of your local paper. Choose four differently styled houses. Describe how you would furnish the dining-room in each house. Figure 15.19 shows you how to do this.

There are many companies now which sell complete furnished rooms, particularly bedrooms and kitchens. Furniture is made to measure and fitted into the space available. This may be very modern 'high-tech' styling, especially for the kitchen, or it may be reproduction-type fittings for a bedroom.

Q 24
Make a collection of kitchen, bathroom, or bedroom planning leaflets. Decide which style of furniture and furnishings you would choose, and list the reasons for your choice.

Obviously, room size is an important factor to consider when choosing furniture and furnishings, but remember to think

Figure 15.19

	House 1	House 2	House 3	House 4
Style of dining suite				
Colour of wood or material used				
Fabric used for dining chairs				
Curtains				
Flooring				
Walls				
Heating				
Lighting				

about the whole house and its surroundings. Is it an urban or rural situation? Do you want the garden to be an extension of the house? The atmosphere of a room is created by the furniture and furnishings, enhanced by the colour schemes, and emphasized by the lighting. It is the individuality of the people which really creates the atmosphere of a home.

Figure 15.20
Design your own room to suit yourself.

How do we use furniture and furnishings to create the character of a room?

We can create and stamp our personalities and individuality onto a room by the furniture, furnishings, flooring, and wall coverings. Different rooms within a home cater for different activities, have different functions for different age groups, and may possibly be combined into one room. Rooms can have several different purposes. A teenager's room may contain a work area with good lighting, yet it will also contain a bed for sleeping. Individuality can be created by the choice of furnishings (duvet covers and matching curtains etc.)

Bedrooms are most likely to reflect the age and personality of the user; different members of a family will have different furniture and furnishings contained within their bedrooms. For instance a baby needs a cot and bright stimulating wallpaper, curtains, and mobiles, but you will have different needs.

Figure 15.21
Bright patterns for a child's room.

Q 25

a Write a list of the different colours of furnishings found in your bedroom. State if colours are co-ordinated or contrasted.

b Discuss in class the effect that different colours and patterns have when placed together. Refer to the colour wheel you drew earlier.

Your bedroom is not just a room to sleep in; you probably work and play in it too. How would you like it arranged?

YOU WILL NEED:

Plain cartridge paper
Drawing materials
Glue
Scissors
Pictures of furniture

1 Discuss what is necessary in order to be comfortable, tidy, and safe while working in your bedroom. You should include a flat working surface, seating and lighting. (You may have learned about ergonomics in Chapter 10.)

2 Make a plan of your own room, or a room which you know. Start with a list of the items of furniture used for the work area, and then put them in suitable positions.

3 Now make another plan of your room showing it as you would like it if money was unlimited.

When you first leave home, you may find yourself living in rather characterless accommodation. If you apply what you have learned in this chapter, you should be able to cheer it up considerably without spending too much money.

15.5 DESIGN PROJECTS

Very few problems have instant and obvious solutions; you often have to bring together knowledge and skills gained from many different sources to help you to solve them.

The four examples of design problems given below link together many of the ideas you have encountered in working through this book, and may also involve some of the knowledge and skills you have developed from *Fibres and fabrics*, *Food science*, and *Nutrition*. If you can develop a way of looking at problems in a 'designerly' manner and learn to work through them to effective conclusions, you should be better equipped to deal with such problems in the future.

In each of the following design projects, the problem is stated as it might be given to you, or as you might find it to be for yourself. Suggestions are then made as to how the project might be developed, following the pattern of the 'second stage' described in section 15.1. The 'third stage' of the project is then up to you.

CHILD DEVELOPMENT: MANIPULATIVE SKILLS
(See Chapters 2 and 3)

The problem
The playgroup leader or nursery assistant has asked you to design and make a toy or learning device for a child aged between three and five years, which will, through play, help to develop manipulative skills.

Development
Assess what skills the child is having difficulty with, decide what kind of toy would help, what materials you could make it from, and how you would do it. Then make the toy.

Notes
Try to observe a child within the target group at play. Children are often ready for new and stimulating toys at this age, and love to practise newly-acquired skills. Simple toys are often the most successful.

SURVIVING AWAY FROM HOME
(See Chapters 4, 6, and 12)

The problem
Young people leaving home for the first time frequently have difficulty in finding accommodation and coping on a low income, and need help in preparing themselves before they do so.

Development
Find out what exactly young people have difficulty with, what sources of information are available, and who can help if they get into difficulty.

Figure 15.22
Some examples of manipulative toys.

DESIGN PROJECT

DO NOT THROW ANYTHING AWAY, EVEN THE FAILURES AND DISASTERS; YOUR COMMENTS ABOUT THEM ARE NEEDED.

DATE ALL WORK.

INTRODUCTION: Start by writing out the design brief you have chosen, giving reasons for your choice. Also what you intend to do in the project (this may change).

RESEARCH: Find out and collect information on your product's history and its place in your culture.

DESIGNING: Show all your ideas/designs/models/tryouts/mock-ups etc.

EVALUATION: At every stage ask yourself 'Why have I chosen this idea or technique instead of another?' Give reasons. 'Does this answer the design brief? If not, why?'

PRESENTATION: This is DESIGN, so present all the above information NEATLY as a DESIGN FOLIO + Index.

DESIGN FOLIO

DESIGN REALIZATION

MAKE YOUR ANSWER TO THE DESIGN BRIEF.

If you make changes during the making record these and say why.

EVALUATION OF THE PROJECT

1. Have you achieved what you set out to do? If not, why?
2. What problems have you found and how did you overcome them?
3. If you were to do the project again, would you do it differently? State how.
4. What do you feel you have learned?

Then design and produce a leaflet or booklet giving guidance on how to survive away from home.

Notes
Think about how much information you should give in this booklet. (People take in and remember a larger proportion of what is written if it is shorter!) Try to use non-verbal means of communication (pictures and symbols) as well as written text.

Figure 15.23
One source of information about accommodation. How useful do you think it is?

BRINGING TOGETHER HUMAN NEEDS
(See Chapters 1, 5, 10, and 11)

The problem
You live in an old house, originally a small two-up, two-down cottage, with a ground floor bathroom and kitchen. Recently it has been extended to give another bedroom and bathroom upstairs and a large family room downstairs. Your parents, your brother/sister, and you have many different hobbies, and the family room is overflowing with these activities. The other rooms downstairs are used as a dining-room and sitting-room.

Last month, granny fell and broke her leg. She is seventy-five, lives alone, and finds it very difficult to cope. After a lot of family discussion, it has been decided that she will come and live with you.

Development
How can you alter your house so that granny can happily join your household?

Notes
You may need to visit an old people's home and look at its furniture for the elderly or disabled. An investigation of local provision of sheltered housing may give you ideas of how old people's needs are met.

Think about ways of making it possible for granny to contribute to family life as well as about the physical problems involved.

Figure 15.24
Low energy houses in Manchester. Energy conservation is most effective if the houses are designed for it in the first place: these ones include a lobby between outer and inner front doors and a centrally located boiler and flue, as well as being well insulated.

MODERN TECHNOLOGY WITHIN A HOME
(See Chapters 7, 8, 9, 13, and 14)

The problem
You have been appointed by a building company to furnish a house at the Ideal Home Exhibition. It must reflect futuristic ideas about technology and energy conservation, and current improvements in methods of home maintenance. It is to be lived in by working parents and their two children aged five and ten years.

Development
Select an area or room in the house and show in your designs how life could be made easier for all the members of the family.

Notes
Remember that rooms belong to people and should reflect their personalities. Colours, shapes, and textures of furnishings should engender harmony and happiness.

Consult literature produced by British Gas, the Electricity Council, and so on. Visit builders' merchants and shops selling household equipment, furniture, and furnishings. Compare what is available and decide what is useful and good value for money.

Figure 15.25
Two war-time utility chairs illustrating good basic design.

Figure 15.26
Designing for the handicapped: this tin-opener can be used by someone with only one hand. How would you go about designing such a thing?

BACKGROUND READING

WE ARE ALL DESIGNERS
Every time we plan a room, decide where a bed or a chair should go, or choose a rug and curtains, we are being designers, whether we realize it or not. The aim of design in the home is to produce a sensible arrangement of furniture and belongings as well as a comfortable atmosphere in which all the members of the family feel at ease. This is the sort of design most people do for themselves, though the articles and furniture they choose are all the work of professional designers, such as the furniture designer who devised the bed and the chair, and the fabrics designer who worked out the patterns on the rug or the curtains.

When it comes to places of work, factories, shops, and offices, many different kinds of designer are involved. The engineers and architects who build factories planned round production lines, or warehouses with a quick turnover, have to concentrate on efficiency of production and delivery. These do not leave much room for considerations of comfort or a peaceful atmosphere.

In the design of shops and their contents, as many as fifty different kinds of designer may be involved. In the case of a big department store, there are the specialists in window design who plan each season's or each month's display to entice customers in. There are the designers of the counters and shelves and display units, the ventilation engineers who have devised and maintain the systems for heating and cooling the store, and the engineers who have designed and fitted the lifts and escalators. When it comes to the actual goods on sale, just about everything has been worked on by a designer — apart from the fruit, vegetables, and meat in the food halls. Even in the case of food, someone had to design and choose the best sizes for the paper and plastic bags in which you take your purchase away.

Did you know that there are professional designers who specialize in designing labels? Think of the problems they have to deal with. They have only a very small space into which they have to cram all sorts of information such as price, size, washing instructions in the case of clothes, or expiry dates for many kinds of food. Ideally, all this has to be readable for the average long-sighted middle-aged customer. In addition, there are codes and marks which cover information of all sorts about their batch, warehouse, supplier, and so on.

Each professional designer has to know a lot about the nature of the materials she works with and the technology associated with them. The fabric designer has to know about the structure of the cloth. The label designer has to be familiar with the different processes used in printing on cloth, plastic, and paper. They have to ask themselves about each product 'how will it work?', just as you, when you make a pottery mug, have to be sure, not only that the handle is comfortable to hold and looks good, but that it will not fall off when the mug is used.

There is more to design than just making or choosing something that you think looks attractive and 'in good taste'. You should now know much more about what makes a successful design and be able to make and choose things with confidence. This confidence may encourage you to seek work in a situation where you can use and develop these skills. Further training will probably be necessary, but working through *People and homes* will have been a useful start.

Figure 15.27
A designer at work.

Index